The Sale is Closed Stop Talking

By

Ira Levofsky

The Sale is Closed
Stop Talking.

Copyright © 2017 by Ira Levofsky

Ordering Information
Quantity sales: Special discounts are available for corporations, associations and others. For details, contact the publisher at the address above.
Orders by U.S. trade bookstores and wholesalers. Please contact Ira Levofsky:

www.Roksci.com
Printed in the United States of America

DEDICATION

In sales you don't get a trophy for participating.
You only win or lose.

Let's win.

Ira

Contents

Acknowledgements

First a disclaimer: If one of the stories in this book resembles you, someone who I have worked for or has worked for me in the past and you are portrayed as a total asshole, it's because you are. The names and situations may have changed.
But you know who you are.

This book is dedicated to all those who hit the street every day with no certainty of income yet overcome and succeed.
There are neither self-help groups nor government programs to show you the road to success nor build the skills to help you ask for the sale.

I've tried everything. Recently I even joined a procrastinators group and will let you know if it helps. We are meeting soon.
The road to sales success is paved with worn out shoes and creative closes.

I hope this book increases your percentages and accelerates your success. This book is dedicated to you.

Cover Photo by Elliott Paul

.

I had a doctor's appointment

Like so many others, my doctor's office is in a three story building full of other medical businesses. As a byproduct of my years of cold calling, even though his office was to the right off of the elevator I turned left as I always do when working a building.

 Walking down the hall I observed that though there were all kinds of doctors, specialists and labs on that floor, the signs on their doors were not the same shape or lettering type. One thing however stood out to me as a common theme.

Each one including my doctor's office had a "No Soliciting" message.

I say a message because there were no formal signs. Simply the words "No Soliciting" made on a labeling machine or even typed on small slip of paper and glued or taped on to the entrance door.

My doctor's office even had a typed page on the frosted glass separating the receptionist from the lobby which read "Salesmen's advances are not welcome here." (But tuberculosis is?)

Now the waiting game began. By the way, I truly believe there is a daily office pool on how long they can make you wait before you knock on the frosted glass, right next to the sign taped to the glass reading "Please do not knock on glass."

Anyway, all of this extra time on my hands got me to thinking. There were nine offices on the second floor, and assuming the building was fairly structured, I guessed that there were twenty five or so offices in the building.

And you are asking yourself "Why do I care?"

Well, just hang on for a minute and you will see.

As a self-proclaimed expert at this sales stuff I devised the following sales experiment.

Here in one building, we have twenty five targets that could really use a proper "No Soliciting" sign. So as not to skew the numbers, we will not include my doctor where I may have an unfair advantage and make it twenty four targets.

Assuming one third of them could be closed on the first call, after my appointment concluded, the experiment began.

It just so happens that there was a Home Depot just down the road and upon asking only three "associates" where I might find door signs, I arrive at the No Soliciting sign rack.
Remembering the low key mannerisms of the Doctors who were my targets, the eight by ten inch bright red and white no soliciting sign was obviously out.

There was however a brownish door colored placard with subdued lettering approximately the size of a candy bar which seemed to be the perfect product for our experiment.

With nine of them on the shelf at a cost of $1.97 each plus a small roll of two sided tape which cost $3.00, the total cost of inventory and supplies including tax was $ 22.18

Unprepared as I was for this impromptu experiment, there were no scissors in the car to cut the two sided tape.

There was however a nail clipper in the sales bag and ingenuity took over. (MacGyver eat your heart out.)

Finally, completely emptying the sales bag and then refilling it with the ready to hang signs, it's time to hit the top floor of the building.

Now join with me on this ride and imagine entering the first office tapping on the glass and when it opens the shrew on the other side says "Can't you read the sign?"

"That's exactly why I'm here," I say "may I speak with the office manager please?"

And when the angry bitch office manager appears at the partially open door she stated that there was no soliciting in the building and asked me "didn't you see the sign?"

"No," I say, "and that's why I'm here. It seems there are salesmen walking around your building (funny right?) and I am here with these beautiful, easy to read yet tasteful No Soliciting signs.

They are only $5.00 each with installation included. I can hang one on your door or wall right now and you will never be bothered by those pesky salesmen again."

Ah the irony, if only Freud were alive we would be in Starbucks laughing about this one.

With a little prompting she comes out to the front door. Then holding the sign up in position covering the existing paper taped notice, and that's all it takes. She goes in the office to get a five dollar bill I removed the shiny white paper from the double sided tape and installed the sign. While graciously accepting payment she is assured by me that once again that her days of being bothered by salesmen were over.

Then by explaining to others in the building how their neighbors, even on that very floor had salesman circling their doors and purchased these signs to keep the salesmen out, the next sale is made. This presentation close combination repeats itself five times in a row until we are out of signs.

Ah, good, I see your paying attention. You're wondering what happened to the other four signs. Well, two of the doctors' offices had three doors and of course needed a sign for each door.

Now here we are with a tremendously successful experiment plus $22.82 profit which is now Starbucks money in the car ashtray.

I hear you. You're not here so you won't get a cup of coffee from this winning effort. But go grab a cup and keep reading. It will be worth the time as your mind will be opened to see opportunities that you would have otherwise overlooked during your down time while waiting and playing a game on your phone.

Now, I have always been a "Sales Dreamer" looking for the next customer in a yet undiscovered market and as young as nine years old I noticed an untapped opportunity.

While in a pharmacy some elderly women from the high-rise apartment buildings in the neighborhood were buying the latest trend.

Hoop earrings with contrasting colors painted on them. You know black hoops with white dots and white hoops with black dots.

Now being New York City, there was literally thousands of apartment's right there in the neighborhood and I wondered how many of these older people just couldn't or didn't want to make the trip to the store to shop. No, this was BI. Before Internet. Why, even touch tone phones didn't exist yet.
Yea, we had it tough back then but even with the new internet shopping of today there is still a huge market out there of prospects, targets that need it up close and personal to pull the trigger and buy something.

Anyway, I asked the pharmacist where he got the earrings and as it turned out there was a local manufacturer's rep who supplied him. Using the money I saved from tips for helping members of the same older people home with their groceries on weekends, I reached out to the local marketing rep and bought a supply of earrings from him.

Then starting on the top floor of the first building, turning left, I began knocking and selling door to door.

In fact I got to see my first naked woman, but that's for my Adventures of Sparky books.

Making a long story short, (yes I can) my door to door earring sales led to my door to door orange bathroom spray sales. Before you know it my success led to a full time (after school and weekends) job and I managed a brick and mortar store in the neighborhood for that very marketing rep who was my supplier.

Well, it was actually a Sears shed on a Gulf gas station parking lot in Queens but to me it was Macys on 34th street.

We sold day glow posters, black lights, rolling papers and other items of the age and though the questions of impropriety, legality and ultimately profit margin closed us down, that wasn't until I learned some very hard lessons about sales and life in general.

At this small busy retail outpost, surrounded by an all new breed of consumer I was confronted early and often with issues about people, personality, honesty, dishonesty money, inventory, and all of the worry that accompanied running a business.

Learning, mastering and overcoming these issues, even at that very young impressionable age helped me to become successful later in life, and in this book many these lessons which still hold true today are passed along to you.

Just because something happened yesterday doesn't mean they won't happen again tomorrow and something that didn't work today with a little twisting and turning might very well work next week.

I know that these bits and pieces of success and failure that you will find in this book will somehow find a way to help you differentiate yourself from the crowd and turn that difference into cash.

It is my sincere wish that the ideas you create from reading this new book be as helpful to your career as they have been to mine.

According to the majority of the hundreds of sales reps who have trained under me over many years, right up to today, my unorthodox sometimes politically incorrect methods have been very helpful to them.

The object is to earn as much as you can being an honest professional and deliver a good life for yourself and your family.

Let us begin, BTW I'm the fat kid in the middle / white shirt

So Why Read This Stuff?

Because you paid for it?

Not a bad reason however we both know that in your past you have bought and paid for a cup of coffee which sucked so bad you left it in the cup or a coke which melted into no more than a paper cylinder of light brown warm water. You then dumped that respective worthless purchase out of the car window, remember?

Yea, I was on the motorcycle behind you. Belated thanks, a-hole.

Now combine that memory with the catalogue purchase which was a piece of cheap Chinese shit and not even worth the trip to the post office to return it, so in the trash it went.

See, you yourself have confirmed and proven through your own actions that just because you paid for something doesn't mean it has any real value to you.

Now other than showing you are intelligent and seeking ways to better yourself, the purchase of this book unfortunately has meant very little so far.

But let's change that right now. The reason you read my books is because you and your Facebook friends (after your referral of course) having read my books will have an all new list of discussion points with which to advance your career, increase your income and enjoy your life.

That's why you bought it. It's my story and I'm sticking to it.

In this book "The Sale is Closed - Stop Talking", I share with you a selection of much of my 50+ years of experience which have afforded me both terrific successes and equally memorable failures.

Yes, this is an honest look at a selling as a career, so within these pages besides the obligatory spattering of amazing motivational success stories, you will also see several examples of horrible gut wrenching failures.

These are self-inflicted failures, which for the most part were brought upon me by me with no outside intervention, and were also very well deserved I'm afraid.

The important thing however, is that almost every time I screwed up I fought my way back and won. Thus learning the valuable lessons, which will now follow in this very reasonably priced learning tool.

These are battle scars from the hard lessons which I have been passing along to my salespeople over the years, which are now being passed to you (and your friends).

Scars from mistakes already made by me and my sales teams, so hopefully once you're aware of them, you won't repeat them.

One such mistake I have made in the past is from when I wrote another one of my sales books, Dinosaur Droppings, Advice from an Old School Salesman. (Amazon)

Though it sells well, I was told by several mainstream companies that even though they would love to buy copies for their entire sales force, it is so politically incorrect (real life) that they just wouldn't take the chance on their employees being offended.

(Offended that is while they no doubt decide what bathroom to use.) But guess what, incorrect, that's the way the world is, and I left the book just the way I wrote it so it would be helpful to you in the real world.

Feel free to also buy Dinosaur Droppings - Advice from an Old School Salesman. (Amazon) and learn something from a sales book while you also enjoy reading it.

Note - If you're offended, give it to someone who wants to succeed.

Now in the interest of reaching the masses so I can hit a broader audience and help more salespeople to succeed, I am attempting to write this book on a more acceptable corporate level.

But rest assured, though I am trying to hit more prospects and sell more books, I refuse to blow smoke up anybody's ass just to make a living and will always tell it like it is.

For example, if you're planning to open a pulled pork stand in front of a Mosque, I will be the guy to point out the potential problems but still help you take your best shot at making it a success.

On that you are assured, I'm your guy. Now let's get down to business.

Good luck and good selling.

 Ira

Choose Sales as a Career

Picture this.

You work for a company owned by a guy who became crazy stupid rich because he invented the toothpaste tube.

He has the type of money that buys handmade Persian rugs with his families' faces woven into them and as if that's not enough his brand new Lamborghini has a mural of a giant dripping toothpaste tube airbrushed on the hood.

Like I said, crazy, stupid money.

Anyway, every day like clockwork, Monday thru Friday at 7:55 in the morning you walk in the door and show up for work like the good soldier you are to do your job, answering the phone in the customer service department.

Quickly swallowing your last bite of donut and final gulp of coffee at exactly 8:00, you line up and you stick in your pointer finger on the bright red light emitting from the time clock on the wall.

With a monotone, simulated human voice you get the same generic sputtering "Good morning" as the girl in front of you in line heard just two seconds before. By the way, she didn't wash her hair again, or at least it smells that way.

Lather, rinse and repeat. Is it really that difficult?

For the next eight hours, save a 45 minute lunch break where you are stuck inside because of the rain, you deal with other people's problems.

By the way, your lunch, the leftover steak and potatoes from last night's excellent dinner at moms, you left on the seat of the train. Now lunch is an undated cold tuna sandwich from the vending machine.

Added to that, you are stuck sitting next to the girl with the smelly hair who ran out to the corner deli, in the rain, for her lunch.

She is now the girl with the wet smelly hair.

Enjoy your lunch.

And with lunch over, after a quick run to the unclean public restroom on your floor, you are back right on time to deal with problems.

No, not your problems like that thump, thump and tick sound coming from your car that morning on the way to the train. Yes the train where you left your lunch bag, on the way to work, in the rain.

But fear not, you will surely get to field the seemingly endless complaints about the toothpaste tube leaking. And the request for ideas on how to get that last little bit out before the tube is tossed will almost certainly help make the time pass quickly.

Like the ice age, quickly. (Which for historical purposes lasted 11,500 years give or take a phone call.)

But believe it or not, you have gone numb to the bull shit and have learned to, well, exist and eke out a living. Then here it comes, the Christmas party, which of course is now the holiday party.

It's a holiday party because the same janitor who didn't properly clean the rest room and took down the American flag in the lobby because he is from Ujerkastan and was offended by its oppressive colors, also objects to all religious holidays.

But he supposedly brushes his teeth and they wouldn't want to alienate a potential customer so they comply with his demands.

And it gets worse as some virtually unknown and equally useless middle manager gets up to make a motivational holiday speech.

In her below the knee length skirt with images of toothpaste tubes on it and a brightly colored sweater with a prominent Christmas tree which she now calls a holiday tree, she clears her throat and begins addressing the crowd.

All smiles she says, "Happy Holidays, if you celebrate holidays that is."

She continues with the ever popular "On behalf of the company, I would like to thank you for all of your effort this past year and look forward to supporting your efforts next year."

The misery continues with "Due to the economy and associated reduced product demand, there will be no pay raises for the coming year. However there is always a silver lining behind every rain cloud and this year is no exception. Each one of you has received a holiday gift envelope as a small token of the company's appreciation for your efforts during these trying times."

Yes, each employee regardless of accomplishment or position in an effort to put the mom and pop store in their neighborhood out of business received a $20 Walmart gift card along with a $1.00 off coupon on the toothpaste of their choice as long as it comes in a tube of course.

Wait a minute. Besides your building janitor has everyone in the country stopped brushing their freaking teeth? How can you possibly receive eight hours a day, five days a week of seemingly endless complaints about, well, bullshit, if there were no products moving off the shelves?

You smell a rat.

No, the girl with the bad hair is standing in front of you again. But something is definitely wrong, you can feel it right down to your working my ass off for this bullshit bones.

Now, everyone in the room, including little Ms. Toothpaste Skirt, knows full well that despite the down market and lousy year, the company owner parked that airbrushed Lambo and flew on a private jet to his yacht anchored off the coast of some warm and exotic island to do whatever you do at times like these in places like that.

You however, are at the top of your pay grade for your position and going nowhere fast, except the train to your car to thump and tick your way home.

Bada Bing, Bada Boom, and just like that, you my friend are at the crossroads traveled by millions of wandering souls every dam day. Someone else tells you what to do and how much you can make doing it.

OK, now shake it off and realize that we were only imagining this nightmare. But, you can use this life experience just as imagined in one of two ways.

1. You can hate the guy but work for him and make what you can based on what their willing to give.

2. You can become the guy and blaze your own trail. Create your own paycheck and be the master of your own destiny.

I chose number two. And that's why I sell. How about you?

Sweat Equity

Going door to door is no longer the only way to find customers but must always be a main play used from your game plan because face to face generates referrals.

Just knowing however that there is low hanging fruit won't tell you about the drooling vicious dog behind the fence waiting for your arrival, hence research is required.

We all use technology and we all do research on computers. Naturally, every company on the market is trying to shove their search engine down our throats.

Siri doesn't understand my NY accent, my Bluetooth dials the wrong telephone numbers and the verbal text messaging in my car repeats back a totally different dialog than I dictated.

Then there's Bing. You click on a topic and get another sub directory and when you click again you get yet another subdirectory. You give up long before you ever get to your answer and go to Google for answers.

I, like our customers want answers, not more and more choices which raise more and more questions. Your target is thinking let me buy something fast and easy so I can get back on with my life. And that's why I say giving me a Google style sales presentation every time helps me earn.

The Google model, ask a question get an answer is what I use in this book and just like all of my books, "The Sale is Closed" hits and hits hard topics that you can never review enough like:

How You Look, How You Smell, How You Sound, How You Listen, How You Talk How You Learn, How You Plan, and so many more. Holy shit, there's a lot to this going out and making a living your own way, huh?

But you already know that because you are holding in your hand a tool that you are depending on to give you some insight on how to increase your income, retain customers and be more creative and successful than the last guy out the door and the next guy coming in the door.

Let's use every psychological, ingenious, creative, truthful and legal method to increase your income, which at the end of the day is after all the only measurement of a sales career.

Remember, technology is in your favor but preparation and execution are required to make you a winner.

Down the stretch there were four horses neck and neck but at the photo finish, Viagra won by an inch.

Let's gain that inch together (no matter how weird that sounds) and win every race. And so we ask…

Is this the beginning or the end?

Well, you already bought the book so it's the end right?

Just kidding, what the hell, you have already paid for it so why not read the book and get the most out of it. By having in-depth out loud obnoxious conversations with yourself, your skills will grow and then you can make it the latest coffee table dust collector if you wish.

BTW, screaming at the book is perfectly acceptable behavior because everyone will think you're on the phone using Bluetooth, so don't hold back.

Trust me, I do it all the time.

And only by reading this book and then discussing it with eight to ten people who you have turned on to it can you decide for yourself if the close of the sale is the close of the mouth. Intense right?

Let's begin with the beginning. (Confucius eat your heart out)

Before we can close, we need to present our wares. Before we can present our wares we need a plan. And before we plan, we need to understand our products and the mindset of the all-important prospects and customers, or as I call them our "targets."

Understanding your target is the easiest thing you will ever do with the help of a few rules and in my experience, I have found that there are only three basic hard and fast rules.

1. It's always about the money
2. They don't trust you, you're salesmen.
3. It's always about the money

salesman
noun sales•man \ˈsālz-mən\
Someone who always takes all of your money.
A person or persons who screws you out of your money while manipulating your mind to believe you are getting what you want.

Example of SALESMAN in a sentence - He was the company's best salesman last year and drives a Cadillac while all of his customers now take the bus.

I know you're asking yourself, "If they all think I'm screwing them, how do I sell to them?" Good question. Getting from prospect to customer is a simple matter of moving them off the thought process they have grown up with. Or as I call it -

Government Cheese

If you're young enough to read this book without assistance but old enough to read it without getting bitch slapped like your reading Girl Scouts Gone Wild under the blankets, then you are affected in some way by Government Cheese.

You see, in the1960's, liberals created an entirely new category of prospects for us to sell to.

Unlike the countless millions of people before them who toiled in the fields or labored over the hot coals of a factory to survive, the government cheese clan decided to take non participatory begging to a new level.

Using the successful business model of toothless haggard beggars in the streets of Paris circa 17th century, when Paris was the largest city in Europe, they evolved them into today's entitlement society.

Here we go class, now put your political correctness hats on the shelf and follow along.

First and foremost back then in Paris the problems with begging were vast.

What with bad weather, poor conditions, lousy hours, smelly clothing and a horrible dental plan, obviously, something had to be done.

That's why when on a particular sunny Saturday afternoon at the fox hunt luncheon, the speaker for the well to do proclaimed, "Poverty unfortunately will probably never go away. But must they all be so, well, poor?"

And from that single question, rather than creating good paying jobs, hundreds of thousands of different assistance plans were hatched to help these poor downtrodden souls on the backs of those who worked hard to support their own families.

As long as the poor stayed to themselves, the well-heeled were happy to put small amounts of their own money and large amounts of everyone else's money into these wonderful new programs.

Wait until they see Obama's farewell gift to America, Section 8 housing coming to a neighborhood near you. Trump, get your pen ready. But, I digress.

Jumping ahead a few years to the early 1960's, when helping people who had become lost in poverty came into vogue once again, the United States government came to everyone's rescue.

Seizing the industrial age invention of processed cheese (Velveeta to you modern day warriors) those who knew more than all the rest decided that it (cheese) was cheap enough, nutritious enough and enticing enough to make it a national welfare program.

And as with virtually every government program, they under thought and over produced.

Next thing you knew, there were chunks, loaves, boxes and cases of unsliced government cheese being distributed not only to the elderly and certifiably poor but to just about anyone else in America who asked for it.

It is also documented that due to the then newly discovered chemicals of the 1960's used in the manufacture of this product, even right now today some fifty plus years later there are warehouses full of bright yellow cheese.

Yes, all across America this cheese will still be there for your grandchildren because it probably won't ever be used, and will never spoil.

And my guess is that there are probably a few perfectly good boxes of Twinkies in their too.

Fun fact – cheese when digested releases casein and casomorphins which have an opioid effect and are addicting. In short – eat pizza responsibly.

Here comes one of those in-depth out loud obnoxious conversations with yourself which make this book worth every penny that you spent on it. If you haven't already blurted out, "Why the hell is this guy going on about cheese?" Go ahead, I'll wait.

And the answer is, the cheese was just the tip of the iceberg followed by thousands of other feel good programs and cumulating as of late with the free Obama phone and the almost free Bernie Sanders Don't Sweat It Never Pay It back College Tuition Program.

Still confused about what I am saying?

I'm simply saying that a majority of people that you have to be face to face with every day to make your living and feed your family have been engineered through the generations to expect it and want it for free. And it makes no difference what "it" is, they still want "it" free.

Go ahead, blurt it out, I know you want to, "Couldn't he have just said that five pages ago?"

Well, yes I could have, but then I don't get to hear you vent in participation. And participate you must because, it's hypothesis time.

Let's take two examples which are as real life as the day is long.

Imagine you are 20 years old and since you were only six, all you ever wanted was a red Ford Mustang. Convertible, hard top, fast back, doesn't matter as long as it's a red Ford Mustang.

To that end you have worked almost every afternoon and six full days every week during the summer for most of the past fourteen years and put virtually all of the money into a passbook savings account.

But this day, the years of toiling in the heat raking leaves and freezing in the cold pumping gas are finally going to pay off.

After a forty five minute bus ride, there you are standing at the Ford dealer viewing a line of used but new to you Ford Mustangs. Three of them are red and you're on cloud nine baby.

Story note - Meteorologists number clouds by size and other factors up to number 10. Cloud 9 is the biggest and fluffiest of the clouds thereby most comfortable looking. Making you very comfortable or "On cloud 9."

Back to the story, the car salesman is busy talking to a girl and her dad who are standing near enough to you so you can hear their conversation.

He is buying her a brand shiny new car for her high school graduation and she chooses, what else, a red Mustang.

You decide that she is the girl you want to marry.

But until then, you need to decide how you will pay the

unexpected increase in insurance cost on your car choice, a hardly used, low mileage, beautiful even with the cigarette burn in the passenger seat, red Ford Mustang.

The sad reality however is that the reward for all of your hard work and high hopes have to be put on hold because what you want is priced higher than you can afford right now and you're not going to settle for less.

And as you head back to the bus stop you are undaunted and determined to accelerate your plan and make this dream a reality. You know that it's time to start working harder and spending smarter, so that sooner rather than later you can acquire your dream car. Spoken like a true winner. Bravo.

After a short wait the bus pulls in and you pay the dollar fifty for the fare then sit down by the window. Right after you sit, three high school aged kids board the bus and sit opposite you.

They didn't pay the buck fifty that you paid but instead they got on for free with their "disadvantaged youth" bus passes.

Wait a minute. These disadvantaged youth kids are all wearing the latest $200+ sneakers and each have a new model cell phone. One guy even has a Samsung 7. He must use it as a cigarette lighter.

Their clothes are all brand new and right in style and in their hands they have those $10 Starbucks drinks with the whipped cream on top. But what the, these kids are disadvantaged, at least that's what their bus passes said.

If they're so disadvantaged, how the hell did they get all of that stuff?

You don't have a new cell phone and your hand me down Jordan's have seen better days. And even though you know your stuff is worn and old because you've been working your ass off and putting every dime in the bank towards your dream car, you're still pissed, and rightfully so.

Man what a kick in the teeth and to make things worse the girl that you want to marry just passed the bus in her free red Mustang dad bought her for graduating high school. Shit, you graduated high school. What a bummer, it seems that everybody gets something but you.

Herein lies the lesson. You see, your anger is making you miss the opportunity right in front of you. It's the big picture, the looming question. Which of course is, if they have all of that stuff then why do they ride the bus for free?

Well, it looks like you did get something after all. You my friend just got a firsthand valuable lesson on Government Cheese and how it affects your success.

You know that the world is full of people who get things for free but also want need or desire things that they can't get for free like the sneakers and cell phones.

These items and millions more, which they can't get for free, makes them in desperate need your guidance to help them acquire what they want and need.

If you grab hold and run with this understanding of the current situation, you will be wildly successful so let's dig a little deeper into this subject.

First of all let's remember that there are always rich daddy's in the world who will spend bucks on their kids. This purchasing group is quite small however and unless you sell Land Rovers in Beverly Hills, the door will probably not swing open often enough with fathers waving checks in the air for you to reach your personal goals.

And where the money comes from, whether they use daddy's money or what's left over every week because they don't pay for rent, food, gas, cell bills or the bus does not matter to you at all.

What matters to you is that you are a finely tuned selling machine, properly trained and comfortable with your delivery.

You are confident, committed and practiced in the proper way. Fully prepared to walk away if the deal is not right for you.

You will sell at the highest possible price, close the deal and then shut up and let them buy.

Remember that your customer base is primarily one of expecting recipients, and there is so much free stuff out there that they will often take what they can and move on.

You must present with conviction that your value as a career sales professional (Would they go to a part time, discount doctor for a circumcision?) and the value of your quality products make the difference.

Your wares are neither free nor discounted and once justified, worth every penny of the amount you demand for them.
It's also important to remember that regardless of the source, there is only so much money for your target to spend before it runs out,

or as I call it, the "money pie".

Those who do not hone their skills but call themselves salespeople are those who are just trying to share a little piece of the money pie.

They try to get any bite of what's left, but they are also the ones who actually make it possible for you to get the entire pie.

When you are the higher price or the non-discountable product presented professionally with reasons to buy that create conversation and agreement, you elevate yourself above the rest. After all, their usually just a guy selling some stuff cheap with little or no preparation nor presentation.

Help the target understand the reasons that they want your product and want it now regardless of price. Once they're on board with that idea they will forget all of the minor purchases they were considering and give the entire pie to you. What the hell, they're going to spend it on something, why not you, right?

They will direct all available money and means to you so they can get what they really want. Once you have them nodding in agreement at a feverish pace you simply need to close the sale and take their money.

Remember: Take all of the available money, all of the time.

Justify it and keep asking for it. No exceptions. A 15% discount on your product is like giving your customer 15% of your income.

Spend your time finding reasons that make your product better not cheaper. Earn all that you can from your quality product and exceptional skills not from a bargain basement price.

One department store sends me near daily emails with 20% discounts. This say's to me that their stuff is not worth what they regularly charge. The grocery store is loaded with buy one get one items and of course everyone knows that you save money if you eat dinner out before 4pm.

Increasingly, every day, everyone, everywhere is being conditioned to get "it" for free or as close to free as they can.

This could make for a very difficult sales situation if not for the fact that your eyes have now been opened.

Opened wide to the fact that rich or poor the world is full of people who want it and expect it and get it for free but there are plenty of those who will still pay for it.

You are the exception to the rule. You are the professional salesman who is there to get past their unreasonable cost expectations and hand them the dose of reality that your quality offering is exactly what they want and need, in exchange for payment of course.

Obviously they know as you know that everything's not free and they have demonstrated they have plenty of money and the ability to pay. And pay they will for those things that they really want, even if they have to finance them.

There are few people who I know that have leased or financed a Porsche or Ferrari and don't constantly bitch about the amount of the payment and maintenance cost.
Yet rather than trade it in for a Prius and save money, they pay

what it takes. So don't feel sorry for them. They want it and you are the one to make that dream a reality.

It's you who stays' focused on the money trail and remember that once you sell them on the need, it's their job to find the money, and they will.

Repeat after me, "It's always about the money."

Repeat after me, "It's always about the money and I need to ask for all of it every time."

Feels good, right?

For a tremendous percentage of this want it free crowd, you are the only person who they will give all of their hard currency to. Why?

Because you are the only one with the balls to ask for it and ask for it all repeatedly until you get it all.

As you can see, we are on the road to success through justified higher pricing which maximizes your income. Also, we agree that we will never lose sight of your value to the target as a professional salesperson.

In addition to the value of your product offerings, you being the real motivator of spending it all will help your target come to terms with spending it all.

From the other so called salesmen, most customers only hear about saving money with a lower price. Not quality and cost justification of a higher price.

Yes, I hear you and agree with you. Everybody else is a discounting hack who doesn't deserve to even be in the conversation let alone affecting your commission check.

Well said.

They will not have your product and industry knowledge nor know how to share it properly.

They have not earned the right to get the sale because they have not put in the hours studying and learning the competitive products.

Since they will not have the depth of competitive knowledge that you have, it will be a simpler task to find their hot buttons and press them with the differences that your product offers.

You want to think about it?

Of course you do, it's more money than you thought you had to spend? That's because it's what you want. It was my impression that you were looking for this, which it has, and this, which it does and this, which it will.

Have you changed your mind about these needs? Are you looking for something additional or different altogether or just cheaper?

You already know that usually it's just the target wanting what you're selling but trying to wiggle out of spending the money, because it's always about the money.

And that of course is where you come in like a pro with "Ok, let me understand, if we have one that does all of the things we discussed that you want as well as these two things that you need that's the one you want but you want it cheaper?

Well just sign here, because this one does all of those things and they don't come at a better value for your money than this one."

Then shut up. Force them to say no. It's very hard to do and a very high percentage of your targets will quickly bust a move and sign just to relieve the pressure.

You must ask for the order and must ask for all of the money, over and over again until they finally break down to sign and pay.

Eventually they all sign or give you the real reason why they won't and you can go right back to work on getting them to commit.

Unfortunately one thing said about salesman is very true. We are so wrapped up in product knowledge and buying signals that when we do a great job, we simply expect the target to buy. Then for some reason, when they don't buy we panic and stop asking them to buy.

It is the rare customer indeed who closes himself and says I've heard enough, I'll take that one. These customers can usually be found in Ferrari showrooms and the Bunny Ranch in Vegas but other than that you had better ask everyone to buy, multiple times until they do.

Having a wonderful performance and taking a bow at the end without the signature does not put food on the table for salespeople.

You must put in the hours, do the legwork and then do the whole job which includes asking for the whole amount every time until you get it.

Remember, they are only talking with you because you're the road to the thing they really want but can't get for free. If this wasn't the case why would they even give you an audience?

I have always believed that anyone who knows I'm a salesman and still invites me in must want to buy something. They are expecting to pay for it and it's only natural for them to want the best deal.

Your job is to inform and educate them while justifying your price point through value, desire, need and whatever emotional response you can find which will trigger the moving of the pen in their hand.

Thereby making them realize that the best deal isn't always the cheapest deal.

Present, justify, close and then summarize and you won't find yourself in line for a box of Government Cheese.

Anatomy of a Salesman's Day

A sales guy made a cold call and no one was available so he handed a business card and a brochure on his leading product to some nameless receptionist who barely looked at him.

The brochure had a price on it so he simply X'ed it out and wrote in big letters "On Sale" to get the curiosity juices flowing. (By the way, we never say "Free" unless you want to pay the college tuition for 126 million disappointed Bernie Sanders fans.)
Then he just ran out of the place (Especially if he had the chili lunch special)

Wait, that's the other guy not you.

You are the one who takes a business card from the holder on the gatekeeper's desk and shoots for an appointment. Knowing full well that if you leave a brochure behind with the gatekeeper and it actually reaches the target, just reading it he thinks he knows your entire product line and no longer feels the need to see you.

You spend a moment and talk with the gate keeper because that gate needs to be opened next time you arrive in order for you to make a living.

You tell her your name (again) and how you just took over the territory for (Company) and you educate her by telling her that you sell a great line of products like (mention two of them)

You ask her if she ever met the rep you replaced or had seen your products at this or any other offices in the building.

You ask her, because you're new to the area, if she could please recommend a good place to eat. Also, it would be so nice of her if she would recommend a time she suggests you go there to beat the crowds.

You pay attention because her answers will expose vast amounts of information about that target and potential competitive information about others in the building.

Additionally you will learn where and when she goes to lunch. Of course knowing the time she usually eats is critical here because when she goes to lunch, she is affording you two new avenues of penetration to reach that prospect which we will discuss in a minute.

Remember, talk with her and take your time, her job is to answer questions. There is no wham, bam thank you mam in selling and the gate keepers have long memories. If they remember that you leave with a simple "not available" they will continue to use it.

Creating confident continuous customers who will buy repeatedly and give you referrals is an exacting process. Whether you close on the first call or the fifth call, getting past or even better gaining assistance from the gatekeeper is an integral part of the process.

Each move in sales is but a grain of sand on a great big beach. (Modified fortune cookie)

Here is a perfect example based on the chain of events we just laid out.

Knowing where and when she eats, you can purposely run into the gatekeeper at the restaurant "Hi Sophia, how are you today? I'm (you) from (your). Thanks for recommending this place, it looks nice."

Of course you are expanding your relationship to one of familiarity and opening the door a crack for your next call.

Or go to her office when you know she is at lunch and say to the lunchtime replacement "Hi, where's Sophia? I'm (you) from (your) is Mr. X in? I just need a minute. Thereby kicking the door open but leaving the Sophia connection alive and well if this ploy fails.

What if the gatekeeper gives you a lead? Close the deal or not, if she gives me a lead I always get a small thank you gift. A ten dollar gift certificate to the recommended restaurant has in the past paid off with many a surprise phone call of additional leads, sometimes months down the road.

We all love leads but remember, hot leads get warm and warm leads go cold and cold leads die.

Should you be fortunate enough to receive a hot lead like "The guy downstairs is looking to buy this from your company," of course jump on it.

But remember, neither the guy downstairs nor the person that recommended you have your knowledge of your product and services so don't ever give a lead the bums rush and never assume he knows what he is buying just because he has seen or used it.

If you simply hand him an order, though he may sign it, you may very well be seen as arrogant or ignorant, or both. And you are.

Every prospect and customer deserves a full features and benefits presentation. This not only secures the sale but opens avenues for additional sales.

What's to say that this lead wants that particular machine that he tried upstairs? Maybe it's the only one he actually ever used. He might need a larger, smaller, more expensive, lease, multiple location solution.

If you just rush in there waiving a contract and signing him up, you risk the phone call "Yours was to slow so I bought a faster one from your competitor."

Yea, it happened to me. This is one of those major screwed up failure lessons which I promised you.

I got a lead and ran in to close the deal like the speed talker on the radio rambling through the disclaimers on the car lease which, by the way, no one actually ever qualifies for.

And not a week after delivery I had the entire unit along with the original packaging shoved up my ass.

As I waddled out of his office, already having spent the commission I offered to him the fact that we had a faster unit as well and he said, oh, you never told me.

It was 100% my fault, 100% my lost money, and 100% my ass.

Do not let this happen to you. It's the single most important part of your job to force them to listen to a full presentation and summary after the closed sale.

In fact, you need to do the summary even if you don't close the deal.

You can summarize as you pack up your sales bag and all of your collateral material scattered all over his desk.

Why is your shit all over his desk you ask?

Because you showed it to him, put it down, and now you get to pick it up. Placing your items on the customer's desk covers up his current work and helps keep him focused on what you want him focused on. Then it buys you more time in front of him while you clean it up.

Imagine the customer has an inventory problem and he put it aside for your appointment. Instead of listening and I mean really listening and participating in your presentation, he keeps seeing that inventory sheet on his desk or his screen.

You need the targets full attention or why the hell are you even there?

Computer screens are the biggest enemy because you can't cover them and don't see what's on them and become a distraction from your presentation. Still there's plenty you can do if the prospect has a computer screen in front of him and it distracts him.

I stop talking as soon as I see them look at their screen. Eventually they realize the silence and look at you. What do you think the odds are of selling to someone who is reading emails while they are supposed to be conversing with you?

Scientifically speaking, they suck.

I have gone as far as to suggest to them that we move to a conference table so I can spread my materials out and he can avoid the distraction of incoming emails and such.

Hey, if it pisses them off, tough.

You're not getting anywhere presenting to someone who is not participating in the conversation. That's not successful selling. It may be good for only one thing, and that is you can cancel your automatic checking account deduction for the Weight Watchers membership.

Because if you keep calling on ignorant assholes like that all day long you will starve to death, for free.

Listen team, I have had customers play Solitaire on their computer while they were supposedly involved in my presentation.

With one guy, I could see the game's reflection on the glass of the Masters Degree framed and hanging on the wall behind him.

I said to that particular guy, "how about you put the jack on the queen and then show me a little fucking respect."

He threw me out.

Yea, I should have suggested the seven on the eight and he would have been able to flip a new card. In any event, I wasn't going to make a thin dime with that guy and sometimes confronting them shames them into being a real interested prospect or even a customer.

Not in that particular case, in fact as I now recall, I was banned from the entire building.

But it's important to remember that even if you blow the sale and may regret doing it, you will always, always regret what you haven't done.

Not trying an idea to get the close, which in hindsight you think might have worked to get that deal will forever gnaw at you.

Asking for, expecting and obtaining the targets attention is as simple as putting on your seat belt. Yet look how many people don't buckle up and die in the crash.

How many salespeople don't ask for the undivided attention of their professional presentation? And then after talking basically to themselves for ten minutes crash and burn right out of their income?

Who cares how many as long as it's not me or you, right?

We worry about ourselves, this presentation, this close and that's why your numero uno baby. Command or demand their attention, if necessary (the Glock is overkill), and then you have taken the first important step of mutual respect, controlling the situation and getting the signature.

Now, let's get back to leaving your stuff all over the prospects desk.

The benefits are numerous. You can review some of the highlighted features and benefits of your product as you stack them up, facing him on his desk.

It will give you the opportunity to mention something he didn't hear or ask the question "What do you need that I didn't discuss with you?"

By the way, this is the perfect time to discuss my use of he and she in this book.

I have spent my career selling predominantly to men so using he is simply a reaction to my past. It in no way is meant to be discriminatory or derogatory to women, so ladies keep buying my books but stop with writing the nasty letters already.

Life is so confusing for an old time chivalrous guy like me. I'm never sure where I can go to the bathroom. The signs on the door have a guy wearing one pant leg and half a dress.

I went to Adam and Eve's to buy my wife a negligee and they changed their name to Adam and Steve's. So if I say I sold him, change it to her if it makes you feel better.

Thanks, we move on.

It is said that a picture is worth a thousand words and not everyone reads at the same speed.

So if you show them a picture, brochure or even physical piece of your product, why not give them time to look at it?

For you, flipping through a brochure or stack of stuff is an everyday event. You have seen these pictures and charts a million times, but your target hasn't. It's all brand new to him so give him the time to understand it.

Everything you show is an important part of your story or you wouldn't bother to show it, so please remember that the person trying to look at it and absorb its meaning might just be a slow reader. You must be patient and give everyone time to understand what you already know.

It might turn out that he is interested in that particular image and willing to dump buying signals all over you. All you need to do is get good at waiting. Showing something is the same as asking a verbal question, you need to wait for the answer or reaction.

Are you paying attention while he looks? Perhaps there is negative body language or facial expressions coming while he is looking at one of your presentation pieces.

You can't just blow by it. You must give him time to express his concerns so you can handle any objections right there and then. If you don't then you will have a suppressed objection and will need a jack hammer to get back to it and close that deal.

Selling is like a racetrack with banking turns, a long straight-away and the checkered flag is the signature.

Selling is not only you against the competition but you against every other thought occupying his mind. Just seconds before you sat in front of him, he was thinking about his wife, his girlfriend, his wife finding out about his girlfriend and who knows what else.

Once you get past everything else and have a direct path to a decision, you need to get every objection out in the open, satisfy them and then pounce.

Additionally every other consideration that wants the money your target has to spend, from the remaining budget to the bean counters, other salespeople and his daughters braces are all scratching and scraping for a piece of the money pie.

Once you're sitting in front of him remember selling is a race against everything and everyone trying to take his dollars, not a race against the clock.

Just take your time and give them the chance to enjoy what you are showing them as if they were sitting in their dream car.

And then once you have let the murmur of the engine relax them and the smell of the exhaust overtakes their senses, you can offer your back to sign the agreement so they don't scratch the paint.

Buyer's Remorse. It's an Evil Mother

One day, three elderly women died and went to heaven. As they waited in the long line to clear TSA they become friends.

When St. Peter came he addressed the three as a group and said "We have but one rule here and as long as you follow that rule you will love being in heaven forever. Notice the ducks walking freely everywhere you look," he said "the rule is that you must be extra careful and not step on the ducks" and away he walked.

The three women figured this was an easy enough rule to follow and headed out to check the surroundings of their new home.

Not thirty seconds later one of the women accidentally stepped on a ducks tail. St Peter appeared, and he was not alone.

Next to him was the ugliest man any of the women had ever seen. St. Peter took the hand of the woman who stepped on the duck and handcuffed her to the ugly man.

Your penalty for stepping on the duck is to spend an eternity with this man and then he vanished.

The two remaining women discussed what had just happened and agreed that they would help each other to be very careful not to step on a duck but it was to no avail.

The second woman took a step backward to allow a duck to pass and stepped on the foot of a duck which was behind her. And instantly St Peter was standing there and again he was not alone.

Next to him was the ugliest man the women had ever seen. St.

45

Peter took the hand of the woman and handcuffed her to the ugly man.

Your penalty for stepping on the duck is to spend an eternity with this man and then he vanished.

Now the remaining woman was very nervous and justifiably so. After all, she had been in heaven for but a few moments and witnessed not one but two women be subjected to an eternity with very undesirable partners.

She devised a plan to shuffle her feet along the ground and not to ever lift them. Though this made getting from place to place very tedious it didn't matter to her because she figured she was there for eternity anyway.

Several months passed incident free when suddenly St Peter appeared before her. And he was not alone. At his side was the most virile, handsome beautiful man she had ever seen and without words he was handcuffed to her then as quickly as St Peter appeared, he disappeared.

The woman was stunned but very pleased that she was to spend eternity with this man. She turned to him and said, "I do not know what I have done to deserve such a wonderful gift as you."

To which he replied, (Come on, you know it. Say it. Say it.) "I don't know about you but I stepped on a duck.

Buyer's Remorse-It's an Evil Mother

You closed the deal and the sale is over, or is it?

This is the perfect opportunity to sell it again and really solidify the deal as well as the customer's (albeit temporary) loyalty.

"Thank you for your business now may I please have your attention for three quick minutes while I review the individual items that come with every purchase which I will be explaining to your staff during the training sessions."

I learned that rehashing what you have already presented shortens the attention span however if you put it in the context of passing it over to others, they listen.

"I know you may never personally be using the (name the product) but my Grandfather once told me that the Master of the ship must know every porthole and turnbuckle."

What you are doing with that action is reinforcing that he is the boss and give him the ammunition to defend his purchase decision when some competition or bean counter comes in and asks why he bought it.

Remember "Buyer's Remorse" it's an evil mother.

Your story may also help him remember something his Grandfather told him. If he shares it with you then you have created a solid, longtime customer.

And make sure to tell him "by the way, when you get a new employee, we will come in and train that employee in the operation of the unit further protecting your investment and reducing productivity loss."

Why? Because it's mandatory that you get back into the customer as often as possible for your very existence. If you just walk away and look for the next victim, some uninterested employee will half train a new hire and they will break your shit.

Next thing you hear is that they bought from your competitor because your equipment was too unreliable or difficult to use. You want to get back in as easily and often as possible to have both you and your product be known by all.

With this said try the old "I'm here to check the equipment" line at the front desk and then have free roam of the location for half an hour looking for new prospects and potential sales. Or develop a liaison in the office with which you can access entry easily. What the hell, your part of the team right?

And on the way out make sure you pop your head in the decision maker's door, "Hi, it's just (Me, I usually use first name only) from (company) just saying hello. I was checking the equipment and training some new employees."

You can add "By the way there are some exciting new developments. Alright if I see your secretary and schedule a quick meeting to bring you up to speed or keep you in the loop? Or do you want me to be talking with someone else?"

Remember that everything changes and at the speed of light. People and positions change. The guy you closed may be gone and his replacement has just been approached by your competition or used a different brand at his last company.

Trust me, this is a real issue. It happens to my sales team every day and managing this familiarity side of the business along with constantly searching for new sales is very difficult and time consuming.

Having the ability to just walk in and not have to do the reception desk dance every time has always been one of my greatest money making tactics.

Being granted fast access allows you to solidify and prospect on every visit without eating up to much of your valuable new sales prospecting time.

Plus the fewer people you need to convince to allow you to get in front of the buyers and users, the fewer potential mistakes you will make with that customer. The more we talk, the more we screw up.

Imagine if you accidentally slipped at the reception desk one day and said "Hey, you know Joe from themail room on the 2nd floor. I saw him in Adam and Steve's the other day buying a vibrating butt plug. Isn't that a riot?"

What you didn't know was that when you saw Joe he was doing every job in the company for a month because Joe is their new CEO. And by the way, his secretary is standing behind you. You probably wouldn't get many more sales there. Crap and that story wasn't politically correct and probably cost me another corporate book sale, huh? But life is really like that, and never seeing one, I don't have another way to describe a vibrating butt plug so corporate HR, get with it.

This is real life going on here so just approve the book and worry about something else like Trumps girlfriends from thirty years ago.

Come on, let's face it, selling is tougher than ever.
Ever since 911, access into a business and entire buildings for that matter have been tightened up like Hillary's email server so in my book and this is my book, every way in is a win.

Brilliance is fleeting but stupid has a way of sticking around so limit the small talk and work hard to be brilliant.

It's also important to remember that the bean counters within the company will always challenge the buyer's decisions to make sure it was money well spent, it's their job.

So do yours. Close the deal, take control and set up the future by reaffirming the decision and limiting buyer's remorse. Proceed as if success is inevitable.

Whatever you do, remember that the quickest way to becoming a grocery bagger is to sell and run to the next opportunity without doing a summary, so don't be a "One and Done" salesman.

Make it a habit to get in, and then get the existing sale, summarize that deal and get a second sale, a referral and a way to get back in all in the same visit.

Also, strive be demonstrative and not a boring talker. The fast way to happy and well informed customers is to show and tell at every sale not just talk at every sale.
Ok, I've talked enough. Come on to the next chapter, I want to show you something.

A Picture Worth a Thousand Words

Remember to spread your stuff out like you own the place. The more you have to clean up the more time you get to do a synopsis, summary and reaffirming of the sale or reopen the dialogue of a failing presentation.

The more physical things to lay out, the better the chance that the target will see something of interest or hopefully even bring up a question or issue that could cause future problems. It is important to remember that you are better off stopping a bad sale than getting a cancellation of a sale you thought was a solid closed deal.

If it's the wrong product and you have the opportunity to correct it prior to the customer cancelling and holding the mistake against you then do it. The odds are you may never get the opportunity to see them to sell them again if they had problems with or needed to cancel or return your past sale.

It's important in today's technological time to remember that if you leave a prospect to try something on their own or ask them to review something on line, you are taking a chance.

When you are not there to guide him, you run the risk of the target getting confused or frustrated with a function or result and giving up. Good luck getting back in to see that guy.

Unless you can do a Go to Meeting kind of interactive presentation, asking the prospect to do self-searching could backfire right in your face.

It's worth pressing hard for a face to face as your in-depth hands

on approach will always certainly stand out in their memory. I am an advocate of low tech presentations because everyone else is killing themselves to be faster and more advanced.
We dare to be different and my presentations, though stone age technology, are a tremendous "mind break" for my targets and make it easy for them to become customers.

In lieu of "Our soup is made with the freshest local ingredients and cooked with an ancient Sherpa recipe acquired in the Himalayas on an expedition in 1903." I believe simple is better and would rather run with a sample and "Soup smells pretty good right? Want to try a taste?"

My teams use "hold in hand" sales aids both physical and visual with not much reading required by the target. This allows each customer to use their own imagination and each salesman to use their own words and personalities to present and close the deal.

It's easy to do, Office Depot will create for you full color 8 x10 screen shots or a full color photo for around a buck. These immediate differentiators make you and your presentation much more memorable and easy to digest.

For another buck I laminate them and that way it doesn't matter who wants to hold them their still fresh for the next presentation. Remember, everyone wants to hold your pictures and each has their own reasons.

Unlike a puppy which everybody loves to hold just because their puppies, many people have poor vision or color blindness or just like to hold what they read in their hands.

You don't care why they hold it, you care because when the next sales guy comes in he won't have all of the great interactive tools that you have for the customer to touch.

Thus making their blah presentation just another reminder of how your superior presentation stands out in their memory.

There is however the real chance that when this book becomes a "Best Seller" the next salesman in the door will also have amassed amazing demonstrative material, so, you have another excellent reason to close that deal "Now."

Here is an important rule about using touch and feel materials. If the sale is not closed and completed when you are leaving and your target wants a copy of a particular piece of material, don't give him one.

[Side Bar -Before starting this practice myself, I actually caught someone throwing the brochure I just handed him in the trash as I walked out the door.]

Today being much more experienced had I seen that, I would have simply asked for it back.

But way back then I simply walked over and dumped the trash can right on to his desk. There with surgical precision, I removed the brochure, told him to fuck himself and walked out the door.

But that was then. You see when I was a young salesman, there were no books like the ones I write, and none of my bosses or managers ever backed me up. They allowed customers to treat the sales guy like shit.

Today, I'm the boss and instead of apologizing for my salespeople

I investigate the problem and if the customer was an asshole, I ask him why he is such an asshole. Then I take my rep to lunch.

Anyway, bringing back the information he asked for, in a day or two does many things. It establishes that you are busy just like he is and you will get to him as soon as you can.

This levels the playing field a bit and lowers his feeling of superiority over the salesman. Let us all remember, if he wasn't interested he would not even be speaking with you.

Bringing something he asked for is an open invitation to get back in and gives you the opportunity to take another try at closing. Never pass up the opportunity to get back in front of your target and never waste it by not asking for the sale.

Also, unless it is absolutely necessary, do not leave anything for him with a secretary or clerk but insist on two minutes to explain something about it with the target.

Only two minutes, honest.

Then do your best two minute presentation and close, close, close.

He is interested or you wouldn't be there. Don't allow time to get in between you and your sale. Time will cool even the most molten metal. Strike NOW while it's hot.

Hey, why don't we just wrap this up now while we're both here? Simple right? What's the worst that can happen? He can say no, big deal, like you've never heard no before.

I can't emphasize enough, even if you have twenty copies of what he wants in the car and seven more in your briefcase, you must resist the urge to go grab one and leave it with him and certainly never his assistant.

Because by the time she gets it back to his office he is deeply involved in a program which Arnold Schwarzenegger told him to get at the App Store.

You really want to wait a day or two allowing the curiosity and fact checking process to run its course so you can use the opportunity to reengage him. Then you have a fresh presentation and try again to close the deal. If the deal already closed then you can use the delay opportunity to let it sink in, solidify the sale, eliminate buyers remorse and get a referral or two.

If however, he wants to make a copy of something that you put in his hand while you are presenting, by all means allow him to do it. Obviously he's interested or why else would he be making a copy.

At that point you try to secure the names of others he is talking with about your product and sell a follow up appointment. Why else would he make a copy except to share it with others, right?

Whether you get the list or appointment you now have a great reason to show up in say, two days with a color copy and some accompanying collateral piece. You can refresh the presentation, go for the close.

Any excuse getting you in the door is another opportunity to close, right? Never waste the opportunity for a face to face interactive visit whether it's a service call or a sales call. And whatever you do, don't show up asking about the copy he made the other day. Expecting him to have retained the copy he made and walking in empty handed is the same as walking out with empty pockets.

You must ALWAYS be prepared to do the sale all over again with your full arsenal of sales stuff regardless of how many times you walk in. Show up fully prepared to present to anyone or everyone and ready to close the deal every time.

Having a business card, something with which to show and demonstrate your product, a sales agreement and a pen are the like the underwear and socks you can't leave home without every morning.

Telling prospects to check you out on the web may be the business method of today however the target may not be able to access the web or understand your program.(For many of us, Space Invaders is the pinnacle of our tech training) In fact he may even have security roadblocks to viewing unknown sites at his desk.

As I am restricted from certain sites at my desk, which forces me to be more productive, many companies have similar security protocol.

You are taking a risk if you ask your target to research, sell and close himself. Your full time job is to get the order, and get it now.

It is very possible that while you parked the car in a five minute zone and ran in empty handed to pick up your order, the real decision maker is sitting in the purchasing office and wants to know how this new thing that their buying works. And you are empty handed.

You never know who else you will meet in an account or the street so it is imperative that you bring everything you need, every time you're going to be face to face.

And remember that personal grooming, punctuality, preparation, positivity, presentation, profitability, perseverance and persistence are all required steps to inking a deal.

Excuse me, I gotta pee.

It's Always the Money

In my career, I have learned that there are three first rules in selling.

Rule #1 - It's always the money.
Rule #1 - No matter how much money they have, they don't want to give it to you.
Rule #1 - It's always the money.

I could probably write an entire book with just this subject and have covered it extensively in my sales books [Dinosaur Droppings (Amazon) And Occupy This (Amazon) Kind of makes you want to read those books also, don't it? This is a subject which needs to be covered every chance we get from as many angles as possible so here we go with another take on why it's always the money.

Don't be afraid of your price. Prices are like phone numbers and everybody has one. You just need to give them a reason to dial yours.

Like when you meet two girls in a bar and they both give you their phone number.

Do you dial the smoking hot blonde waitress who needed to borrow a dollar for pretzels or the moderately unattractive one who snorts when she laughs and her father is chairman of the board of a multinational company whose jet she is using to go to the Hamptons for the weekend?

Believe it or not this is the same question your prospect is asking about your copiers, insurance or trash removal service.

Are looks enough? Does he want to buy the best future or just to get by for now?

Hopefully you are the most expensive in your market and you can put great quality, performance and product superiority distance in-between you and the competition therefore justifying the higher price.

This means you can and have articulated the fact that you, your company and your product have the best quality, most solid infrastructure, top level of service, newest technology, most advanced research and fastest turnaround to bring it all to market.

And now the fun part, everything I just said could apply to a

MULTILEVEL SELF CALIBRATING DIGITAL SCALER, RATEMETER RADIATION MONITOR
or a
NEW COUNTERTOP DISPLAY WITH 200 POCKET SIZE PACKAGES OF GUM IN BOTH PEPERMINT AND WINTERGREEN FLAVORS

Selling past the money is all about painting a visual picture for your customer which helps them make the decision as if they were seeing and touching the value of your wares right there, right then.

But before you can get to this miracle of successful selling, the close, you must first get your two way presentation conversation down right.

Then once you get it flowing right, it matters not what your price is because you have featured and benefited your prospect into a head nodding fury of a conversation and with pen in hand he is clamoring for more places to sign.

In other words, they will ignore the snorting.

To most this means practice, and I am the first one to say you don't become a fighter in the middle of the fight. If you train incorrectly, then you get better at pulling yourself off the canvas than putting your competition against the ropes.

Everyone who has worked with me, for me, around me, listened to my Sales Mojo radio show or read any of my books knows what's coming next. The single most important lesson you can learn, not only in selling but life itself is,

Practice makes Permanent.

Practice makes perfect only if you use a perfect model but if you practice from a flawed model you will come out permanently flawed.

In other words, shit in, shit out.

It is hard to nearly impossible to forget wrong words, processes or methods which you have practiced and molded into your presentation or everyday life.

That's why your mother always told you to stand up straight. I myself can still hear my mother saying "Quit pulling on that thing." Oh sorry, wrong memory.

The muscle and mind memory of walking droopy shouldered and hunched over doesn't go away once it is the acceptable position to your brain.

Just check out people in the street. You can easily pick out those whose mothers never told them about their posture.

I give exception to Quasimodo, he couldn't help it.

Historical note – When Quasimodo fell off the Notre Dame church and the crowd gathered, a guard called out "Does anyone know who this is?" Someone from the crowd responded "I don't know his name, but his face rings a bell."

Anyway, practice is a must but practice makes permanent so make sure you are using the right ingredients for success.

If you are one of the lucky few who has a sales manager or sales trainer who gives a shit about your success and not only their spreadsheets and reports, push that person for some one on one training.

Not bullshit group roll-play but real conversation over coffee about the battlefield out there and his or her experiences fighting the big fight and winning business.

I'm referring of course to the battle for Success.

Also to reach the level of success you strive for it is imperative that you get yourself into the marketing and advertising departments of your company. Once you do ask them why they chose certain aspects of your product to feature and others to ignore.

There amongst those who live and breathe your products, you will learn of the successes, failures, problems and growing pains which now make your product what it is.

Knowing the history makes it easier to prove you're the best investment on the market. Understanding why your product had many changes throughout its lifetime will allow you to have much deeper conversations with your target and take you away from the information in print, "off the menu" if you will.

This intimate knowledge of your products will establish with your target that you are the expert and the best person to trust with his purchase decisions.

It's refreshing for buyers to hear about things that weren't exactly working as planned and corrected through trial and error. This inside knowledge also offers you the opportunity to discuss the many improved things in the newest model which we are discussing today and they are.

It's even more refreshing for a prospect to have a professional salesman who isn't afraid to discuss the somewhat checkered past of his products and services so the target knows he is dealing in reality not smoke and mirrors.

Transparency, as the politicians call it. But instead of making excuses you deliver it and explain how things were fixed and now there are no hiccups with the product you are proudly selling, so sign here.

Now if there is nowhere to get information which created the sales material or you can't find the reasons for past success or failures you will need to build your own knowledge base.

The biggest problem here is, that like anything which you are unfamiliar with, without a past user you have only a brochure to learn from. In cases like this you chance learning lots of wrong information very quickly and put yourself behind the eight ball from the break.

I have always been a fan of finding a local end user of my product or service or even the competitive products and services.

Simply offer to buy that person a cup of coffee if they would give you a few minutes and explain this new product that you now need to sell from only this brochure.
Or, if a competitive user, give me some firsthand user data on what their using for comparison purposes.

By telling your expert that you wouldn't want to misrepresent either product and certainly recognize and respect his expertise in the area, they will usually give you a little time.

Remember, everyone considers themselves an expert at something and everyone likes to teach.

If your chosen expert likes what you're selling then there is no harm in a simple close like "So, you want one? You can be my first customer."

Though in this situation it would be tacky to close too often I think it is perfectly acceptable to milk this great information source for potential buyer references.

Remember you don't have your experts experience and education nor want to mislead anyone by describing the product or service incorrectly. Tell your new teacher that you need the advice of an expert so you can do the job honestly and correctly.

Here is a simple example of why you want the advice from someone already in the game.

Mechanics often become tool salesmen. But it's the mechanic lying under a hot oily mess of an engine who first realizes that the manufacturer came out with a new star shaped nut which needs to be removed.

The entire job is now stopped and cannot be completed without this brand new nut removal tool.

Yea the fact that he needed this wrench might have been in one of the hundreds of new daily bulletins the mechanic is supposed to read but ignored. But it doesn't matter now. He needs the wrench.

It's also possible that the salesman did read all hundreds of his bulletins on new products coming down the pike but how was he supposed to know that this single wrench could be his springboard to success. After all, it was just another new wrench added to his product line.

So making cold calls on both customers and noncustomers asking "What's new" he learns that this new wrench is the lynchpin to a landslide of business.

As more cars have issues which need this new crazy shaped nut removed, he can be there with the solution. This salesman needs to hurry and call his company and find out about inventory, delivery and price and get orders for this wrench.

Of course if he could get his hands on one wrench to temporally help out that mechanic with the stalled job he would have a customer for life and most probably referrals to all of the other mechanics in that shop.

He could probably even ask for a copy of the manufacturer's bulletin (I know I would get it and have it laminated for presentation purposes) to carry door to door while he sold that new wrench to every mechanic he could talk to.
Or if they weren't inventoried yet, take deposits on the limited inventory coming in next week.

And by the way, this purchase qualifies you for our low interest payment plan on a full tool set.

I'm getting all excited here but let's get back to why you need someone who uses or knows in-depth your product to teach you the foundation of your selling presentation.

Also a quick overview from an end user of your new item will give you buzz words, areas to stay away from and cost valuations you need to get started and get started selling the product correctly.

One wrong statement can bring up a question or objection to which you don't know the answer and then the customer is an iceberg and you're the Titanic.

All of this correct input from your end user combined with your good question asking skills will build your knowledge base and in turn a solid platform from which to sell and be successful.

Don't shake your head. Everyone loves to teach. There is no bigger honor in life than someone asking you to pass the torch of knowledge. This is why I run sales teams. This is why I write.

Someone must help others develop their skills to the point where they can go forth and prosper with no fear of price or competition.

And once that newly developed skilled sales professional reaches the top, hopefully they will step in and continue the teachings to new generations of wide eyed sales reps so us old timers can live in Florida and write books.

Smarter Than the Average Bear

That's right Yogi.

If there is a pick-a-nick basket out there somewhere, besides you, there's plenty who want it. The one who actually gets it all comes down to ingenuity. Yours. Let's get right to the meat of the matter.

For this we travel back in time to jolly old England.

Like all governments, the British have always been a fan of taxes. But you already know that, because if it wasn't for the taxes on the Americas, the whole Tea Stamp Act, Paul Revere thing in the 1700's, we would all be driving Jaguars on the wrong side of the road today.

Anyway this tax discussion is the perfect way to cover the topic of if they want it they will find a way to get it. In the mid 1600's thru the year 1747 (not long before our little tax falling out which we called the American Revolution) England was in the midst of a building frenzy and brick row houses were going up at a feverish pace.

The English government sees this prosperity happening and says, "Wait a tic. We need to get our share" and just like that the Window Tax was born.

You heard it right, a Window tax. The British government taxed people based on how many windows they had.

They no longer needed to go door to door and perform a head count (our Census) to get their lion's share of everybody's everything. The needed only to take a leisurely ride down the street and charge them tax based on how many windows they had.

Now most houses built in London for instance were multifamily or row houses and with lots of units comes lots and lots of windows so no matter how poor you were, your window tax made your pocket that much more empty.

This was such a simple way to take so much from so many that soon Scotland and France joined the party and put in a Window Tax of their own.

At first, if there were ten or more windows in your house you were taxed. But like all governments, England's got greedy and in 1747 they lowered the taxable window count to just seven.

And if you like your windows, you can keep your windows.

Well as you might guess the English citizenry wasn't going to take this lying down.

They refused to sell their Bits and Bobs to pay more tax. But in lieu of telling the government to Get Stuffed and Bugger Off (Such a colorful language those British) and then winding up with their head and arms locked in the Pillory they needed some divine intervention.

That's when salesman's ingenuity stepped in turning needs into wants and wants into needs.

Historical note - The practice of selling and creating wants and needs dates all the way back to the recordable Stone Age. Cave drawings have been discovered bearing crude but understandable depictions of early man trying to get a better price from early salesmen.

Another cool fact – Today, December 2016 there is an active tax in Brussels Belgium called the Dance tax.

No kidding around here, if you go out to a club and dance then you pay the equivalent of 40 cents tax. So drink up, dance and pay.

But back in the mid 1700's a brilliant construction materials salesmen, we will call him Fred and his tradesman, we will call him Barney hatched a marvelous plan.

Fred and Barney went door to door and sold bricks and paint for the homeowners to make the windows simply, disappear. It was a brilliant sales pitch. No windows, no tax.
Yes, they sold the idea and corresponding materials to simply brick over the windows and also provided the installation of these bricks

for a small additional fee.

Fees mind you which would be quickly recovered by future tax savings.

Sign here.

One by one virtually every home on every block in every neighborhood was covering most of their windows and painting the new brick to match the exterior walls.

Cool historical fact – These buildings with the bricked over windows are still visible today in older sections of London.

Now just to close the circle of the story, in 1766 due in part to Fred's tremendous sales program success, the number of houses with seven windows or more was reduced by two thirds which contributed to the government almost going broke.

Another effect of Fred and Barny's closing ratio was the unintended health issues said to be caused by living without ample light and fresh air due to lack of windows. They included cholera, smallpox and typhus just to name the big three.

As you probably guessed, these additional problems associated with bricking over the windows prompted the tax to be repealed and then the British government immediately started looking for new ways to make money without actually doing any work. This need for fresh revenue was probably a catalyst for the whole Americas Tea Tax Revolutionary War thing.

Now don't get me wrong, many profited from the window tax. Including our two enterprising entrepreneurs, Fred and Barney who made a killing and went on to buy everything they ever wanted. The boys built huge homes with 25 windows each and filled them with all the best things money could buy.

And just think, all this success came from pure raw ingenuity and effort because of a tax which created an idea which then created sales which created commissions.

And here we are at the beginning of the story again.

But what does it all mean?

Are you thinking what I'm thinking?

That Wilma and Betty don't seem like the type of girls who need 25 windows?

Do you think the girls are still yelling Yabba Dabba Do every time they clean those gynormous homes or do they silently long for better times again so they get their maids back?

Since all of the boys collective wealth came from a narrow product line in an industry both created and destroyed by government greed, which incidentally disappeared faster than the Livestrong bracelet, Fred and Barney needed to find a new gig to survive.

Just what were Fred and Barney going to do to earn money they needed to pay for what they had and also for the things they still wanted?

After all, who could have predicted this outcome? You really can't blame the boys for not growing their product line beyond their flagship window blocking because they were working as fast as they could to make as much as they could.

Besides, they had to beat the competition that was already nipping at their heels.

Every day new companies were springing up covering the windows with that new cheaper Chinese brick that hit the market. And their choice was either expansion or survival.

Remember, eventually due to a virtual guarantee of cheap to market competition, every business is always caught in the growth vs. survival quagmire.

quag•mire
noun
A foreign hoard that sells cheap shit which begins sinking businesses as if they were in quicksand.

Example of Quagmire in a sentence:
"Those Chinese brick laying bastards were creating quite a quagmire making our margins smaller and survival more questionable every day."

To that end we ask this simple but most important question. When you have a flagship product, how do you survive once the thrill is gone?

First, before we worry about the end we need to focus on right now.
You must close every target you can get in front of, thereby

making you crazy successful and stupid rich which supposedly eases your day to day stress.

Yea I know what you're thinking, money brings new problems, but that's not the stress were talking about. We're talking about how a target can always spot a salesman who needs the sale.

Like the guy in the Schwarzenegger movie who was supposed to be in Arnold's dream but then he sweats. Once the bead of sweat starts rolling down his cheek, Bam.

It's no different for our targets. They see every little twitch, hear every mistake and nervous statement and they know when you really need the sale. Then here they get all powerful feeling and start with the demands for discounts and concessions.

They must want and need what you sell without any distraction caused by you.

In fact, let's take a break from making your target both need and want you as well as want and need you and discuss you being you.

Assuming that you are a true study of your product and services, know your company's history and have a handle on inventories and delivery schedules then you are already light years ahead of your competition.

Let us keep in mind that only two out of ten salespeople are truly successful but various factors like some ass wipe being in the right place at the right time can still steal your order.
So if you have nine competitors, eight of them are a nuisance but could still be right place right time and one is a real threat.

You need an edge to be the top dog and get the deal to close first time or be the one to chase. And amongst other things, a bead of sweat won't help you.

Cool, confident like the international spy walking into the bar, that's you. (And Sparky in Adventures of Sparky – The Pirate Wore Wooden Shoes. (AMAZON))

But is it? Let's talk for a minute about what a target really sees when you walk in the door.

Did someone order the fish?

Just what did you have for lunch?

Are you neat and presentable? Even if you wear golf shirts with your company logo on it like so many companies do, you still need to appear professional and very successful.

Is your shirt pressed and are your pants clean and pressed?

Wash and wear doesn't necessarily mean shake them and wear them. Take a look in the mirror and if you don't look like someone you want selling to you, take the time to fix it.

Are both the top and bottom of your shoes clean?

Walking into someone's office is no different that walking into someone's home. Respect is required. Leaving a footprint trail on the customer's carpet will be a constant reminder of what an inconsiderate slob you are. Good luck closing that deal.

How are your fingernails? Were you working on the 73 GTO this weekend? (Lucky bastard)

Do you have all of your presentation materials with you?

Oh, you use an Ipad? Not having the picture or descriptive brochure with you of the product(s) you are selling is Murphy's favorite law of guaranteed failure.

Your Ipad will fail to turn on and you can't show the product so you ask to show the product to your target on his desk top screen and now here comes Murphy's Law in spades.

Yes, you type in the site for your 3D adaptable widget but what comes up is the last site he visited. And wouldn't you know it's the BJ scene from Debbie Does Dallas. In 3D.

You may laugh but it happened to me. (But there was no 3D back then) Good luck closing that deal or getting to watch the entire movie, I didn't do either.

Lack of preparation, like having a simple paper to present from, leaves you forced to describe what you're selling with only words and as we all know, a picture is worth a thousand words.

We also all know that no target will sit through a thousand words. This boys and girls, is why I laminate 8 x 10 color photographs of key products for my sales teams to carry in their sales bag.

My salespeople (of which you are now a member even if you borrowed this book) can present on a moment's notice, on the bus, in the parking lot or even in the men's room if need be. (Wash your hands first)

This is assuming they have practiced correctly because remember "Practice Makes Permanent." They have a pen (that works), a presentable clean contract along with a shiny new business card and a winning "do this all the time" attitude.

Then and only then will they have a very high percentage of being a winner, every time.

I would like to take this moment to thank all of my sales teams over the years and welcome and wish all of you newcomer's tremendous success.

When you do well, it means that I did well.

Winning at the game of selling is actually quite simple for a skilled outgoing individual such as you.

Selling is all about a successful appearance, attitude and being prepared combined with smart and hard effort.

Selling means you have no income cap. (And if you do, either renegotiate your deal or find a new company.)

Here are some highly recommended basic questions you should ask yourself before you go out to sell every day.

Do you have fresh contracts and agreements?

Old dog eared contracts create the appearance that you rarely use them. The target figures that they get beat up in your briefcase because their always getting shoved back in, unsigned of course.

Suggestion: Keep all papers that require a customer's signature in a folder so they are always pristine.

If you always get customer signatures on your ipad, it is highly recommended that you have some printed agreement copies in your bag for that one time when Murphy comes to visit and your ipad screen stays black.

Are your business cards bent?

Personally, this is one of the things I hate the most. Your business card is a representation of not only you but your company and product. Business cards in societies like Japan, are so important that they are presented with two hands.

Try two hands, it peaks your customers curiosity and you may even get to explain why you did it starting that all important conversation.

Yea, it's just another way to differentiate you from the masses and win the game.

Do you have a pen?

I used to insist that my sales team present a pen along with the agreement for signature until I found that asking the target for a pen was a great trial close and an easy way to transition the pen and paper into his hand for the signature so this one is an individual call.

But a word of advice, have a pen hidden in your bag anyway incase the target doesn't have one so you can dig and say "here it is" and hand it to him.

What did you have for lunch?

Talking to a target with your breath stinking like curried lamb with raita sauce and red onions from the Indian restaurant on the corner will probably cause your target to think about nothing but "you stink" and forget everything else you said or did.

When his partner comes in at the end of the day and asks who that salesman was, instead of saying "he had an amazing solution for our problem, let me show you" the answer will be, "some guy whose breath smelled like a camels ass, I couldn't wait for him to leave."

Same goes for cologne and fragrances.

If your shaving cream, hair spray, hair gel, deodorant, cologne, laundry detergent and fabric softener are all fighting for the number one spot of what you smell like today, take my word for it, trash them all.

If the target thinks you were in a terrible accident and got hit by a truck full of Hai Karate, and then you were thrown through the window of an Indian restaurant in the accident, his attention to your presentation may be as difficult to hold on to as one of Hillary's emails.

As a successful professional sales person, you must think and be sensible about how you approach your simplest decisions every day.

Not unlike a surgeon who goes through the ritual of dressing and scrubbing before surgery, you need to pack your briefcase, take stock in how you look, sound, smell and the amount of success you project for that day before you walk in the targets door.

What we are really talking about here is the fact that every face to face is an opportunity to increase your income and every step of this process is equally important.

Regardless of your physicality, whether you're the old you or the two for one double quarter pounder you (Hey it happens to the best of us) to be prepared you must look prepared and to be successful you must look and act successful.

This brings me to another very important requirement for success, I call it

The First Kiss

There are certain things in life you can hang your hat on like virtually every romantic novel, country song and engagement ring commercial has one thing in common. The first kiss.

What an unforgettable moment, the adrenalin, the nervous feeling in your stomach, the alcohol. Ok, whatever, nod if you agree that as a rule, the first kiss is either a deal maker or deal breaker.

And in sales it's no different. The first meeting, whether it's an introduction, in the street or on an elevator, a cold call or scheduled appointment, the first few seconds is make it or break it time.

This is the small capsule of time where your target gets to size you up and decide if they trust you.

Did you check your attitude at the door?

Don't kid yourself, your prospect knows when you had a fight with your wife or the credit card company called about your late payment so put on that successful happy face long before you hit his door.

Do you have a firm handshake? A neat appearance? What did you have for lunch? Do you smoke? (That's a big one, breath mints don't remove the stink from your clothes and prospects almost always notice when you spit a big green cough induced lugie into their trash can)

These actions, sights and smells are all locked in the targets memory banks within seconds of this first meeting.

Now recently I read an article and followed the blog discussion from a supposed sales expert who said that both customers and salespeople are nervous and uncomfortable at the first meeting.

Their obviously clueless as to what a trained, well-groomed successful sales pro with a polished fifteen second presentation is capable of.

Perhaps they should get off the blog and get out on the street.

It's like when a person is meeting a big dog for the first time and the psychological experts are trying to figure out who is more nervous the man or the animal. They always ask the dog.

Successful Professional Selling is not something that can be comprehended from the outside looking in. Selling is an art form, a discipline not unlike martial arts which requires dedication and practice to become proficient and ultimately successful.

An expert bomb technician, who became one by reading about how to diffuse a bomb, but never felt his heart beating in his fingertips while the clippers cut the wire, is no expert.

Trust me when I tell you that I have 50+ years of sweat, tears and lessons learned and still feel the excitement pounding when I first meet prospects.

And then for the close its sheer exhilaration when the pen hits the paper. But for us sales pros it's not uncomfortable, its awesome.

Be the true sales professional, disciplined, dedicated, honest, and confident and enjoy every sales call and selling opportunity like it was the first date.

Strive to clear the way for that exciting first kiss.

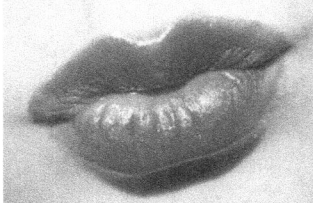

Witches and Liars

The farmer said to the cop "I was just helping it over the fence"

Lucky for him that sheep don't talk, and they lie when they do.

If only Freud were alive today he would spend a month on that one. We however can cover this subject in but a few pages. No, we are not entering into a discussion about summer love but one about honesty.

It's really quite simple, tell the truth, all of the time.
Tell the truth even when it's unpopular and when you lose the deal because of it.

Always justify the truth when you walk away without the deal and you may just win that deal back, down the road. Then avoid saying I told you so. (I know it's hard)

I know that sounds odd, but when you speak frankly and genuinely, or is it speak genuinely to Frank? I lost my place.

Oh yea, when you're in a two way conversation and ask the customer whether he wants the truth or some smoke blown up his ass, he will usually opt for the truth. If he wants the smoke, well that's your call.

Anyway, there are few things more satisfying than having a customer call you and tell you that the other guy lied to them and couldn't deliver what they promised him.

That very thing happened to me the other morning and I got to add a few penalty commission percentage points to the deal that I closed. With no argument I might add.

I'm not talking about pushing the delivery date to the limits of what's possible because once the deal is signed there is a grey area that we do not control.

I mean of course that if you know you're out of the blue package and they are going to ship the red package you had better fess up when the paper is inked. Don't try to back sell the customer after the delivery of a warehouse full of the red ones hits his loading dock.

The problem here isn't that the customer can't use the red package, it is that you didn't tell him in advance that red was coming even though you knew dam well there was no blue to be had anywhere. The bigger problem is that he might think either you or your company is incompetent.

And the biggest problem is that when it happens more than once, you and your company are now definitely grossly incompetent.

Not telling the whole truth upfront will lead to a customer telling you that your company keeps screwing up so they went to the competition.

Earnings note – Any time you can get a big order take it. Why you ask? Go ahead and ask. Ok, I'll tell you why.

Because just in case your customer decides not to prosecute, oh wait sorry wrong gross incompetence.

It's because even if your customer overlooked the past deliveries which were consistently late or for the wrong color product, you run the risk of your competition getting one over on you, taking the account, and then you're not making any more future money with that customer.

Believe it or not, you are not the only one acutely aware that blue outsells red.

In fact, while you were stuffing your customers shelves with the only package you could keep in stock, your competition was busy with their newly developed think tank creating the latest fad.

By gathering a group of one hundred people from the ages of six to sixty six, after a double blind taste test they discovered that consumers would buy a hybrid packaged blue and red product at an alarming rate.

What this means to you is that when you finally have blue packaged goods in stock and go bounding happily into your sure thing sale, you know, the customer that always buys blue. Then you get kicked square in the teeth.

You are handed the latest hottest selling blue and red spiral packaged product from your competition. The same brand new package that your ex best customer just signed a long term, stuff the warehouse till it bursts order and no longer has a need for you.

Surprised?

You shouldn't be.

The dollars you earn today are the only guarantee.

If at any time you have the opportunity to close the sale, slam the door shut and take as big an order as possible preventing your competition from finding any space on the shelf for a "let's try it" order. This goes for every product or service that you sell.

After all you have a hard to get and always on the brink of extinction product that is finally in stock and it is your responsibility to bury him in it.

Why?

Because you can, it's a hard item to get. Make it a practice to always get the most from every situation, highest price, plus referrals and most importantly always tell the truth.

Plan B - After a disaster like losing a big customer, all is not lost. Even though you lost the big deal you need to shake it off and go make all of your smaller customers into bigger deals.

Your competition can't get to everyone so you need to find all of the available customers and sell them mass quantities, now.

If they mention this new spiral product they heard about you simply tell them that your company has positioned itself to supply the "proven" product. The blue ones that always fly off your shelf and you suggest he load up now in a big way while the inventory is still available.

You must either go on the offensive or practice asking "Do you want fries with that?"

"Mr. Customer this blue package is very hard to get. But you already know that because red was substituted to fill your last order. In my opinion, you should take advantage of the quantity of available inventory right now before its gone Again."

Bam, big sale before the competition gets in with their new spiral. The customer gets what he wants and you get yours. Détente, with a commission twist as it were.

OK, this was a great example if I say so myself, and I do but we have some more blank paper so let's go with one more example.

I'm sure unless you have lived a fairytale life and have never been lied to you will agree with the rest of us in the civilized world that everyone hates to be lied to. As far back as time and testament, this has been a true statement.

For this example we need only to go back in time as far as 1692 and the place Salem Massachusetts. Of course you know where I'm going, the Salem Witch Trials.

I chose these hated individuals because they exemplify the only two results that are possible from being a witch or being a salesman caught in a lie.

Let us first clarify some important facts.

You can be fat but lose weight. You can stutter but can get speech therapy. You can go bald but get a hat. But once a liar, always a liar.
When I was a young boy, my mom pounded that into my head and one day it made sense and of course you know the reason so we won't get into the grizzly details.

The following are the above negative characteristics about people which can be explained away and even turned into a positive.

He's the fat guy with the beard. Oh no, he lost a ton and looks great.

That guy was really hard to understand when he talked with a stutter. No, he went to some therapist and now he sings everything he wants to say and it's actually kind of cool to talk with him.

That salesman went bald so young. I didn't notice, he was wearing a nice hat.

And now the one you can't defend.

Yea, I used to deal with him but he lied and we got screwed.

Oh, you can't trust him? What a useless piece of shit. I won't use him either. Thanks for the warning.

What other ending could there be?

He doesn't lie any more.
He told me he quit lying.
Well, he only lied because his product was inferior.
What do you expect, he's a salesman. (Personally, I hate this one)

Take it from me with 50+ years knocking on doors and hundreds of sales reps working with and for me, nothing works, once a liar always a liar.

OK, now that we have established our facts let's try the following experiment. For our purposes, we will take this dreaded word Liar of today and substitute the equally dreaded word of the 1600's, Witch.

In the 1600's, if you were accused of being a witch, you were brought to trial and at the trial they simply asked you if you were a witch.

If you said yes, they burned you at the stake.

If you said no, figuring you were a liar they tied your hands and feet then tossed you off of the town bridge into the raging river rapids and rocks below. Then if you survived being thrashed around for one hour in the freezing rushing water they would bring you back to court and ask you again if you were a witch.

Why?

Because everyone knows that witches lie, that's why.

And since they didn't believe your innocence even after surviving the torturous burden of proof, they drag you out and prepare to throw you off the bridge one more time, just to be sure.

Usually by this time knowing that you will surely drown and die, in your weakened state you agree that you are indeed a witch and beg for mercy.

And then they burn you at the stake.

Can anyone in the class tell me the upside here?

No, because once a witch always a witch and once a liar always a liar. And those who are certain that you are a liar, or a witch won't stop until they have proven it.

What is the moral of this story?

Make an honest living, carry your head high and sleep reasonably well at night as long as tomorrow isn't the last day of the month.

Point well made, we move on.

Interpretation

Let's start with a simple question.
How many spaces are there in between your toes?
Hey, put your socks back on, that's cheating.

No matter whom I ask, from five to fifty five years old I rarely get
the same answer.

Please note I didn't say the correct answer because based on an
individual's interpretation, all answers are correct.

Are their four?
You say six because of the spaces on the outside count.
And yet another says eight because they have after all, two feet.

Then there's the nine and ten crowd culminating with the ever
popular Adams Family favorite two, ten, eleven.

What does this all mean besides the obvious fact that Uncle
Festers' best trick was the one with the glowing light bulb in his
mouth?

It means that if you ask a question which does not have a definitive
answer, you will get a multitude of answers, which by the way,
may all be the correct answer.

Is this a bad thing?

It depends on whether you are trying to get agreement and close on
a particular point or whether you are fishing and need to pick a
direction to go in.

Questions should always produce answers that help you continue selling and gaining commitment to the ultimate goal, the close. In any event all questions are only your second most valuable tool.

Can anyone in the class tell me the most valuable weapon in your the sales arsenal?

Yes you in the plaid pajamas.

Your Glock?

Well, perhaps, but only if your selling plywood in Baltimore or Ferguson.

Listening is your most valuable tool and in the answer to every question you should hear bits and pieces of the next question and ultimately the way to lead the prospect down the winding path and signing on the dotted line.

Questions or interrogatories for those of you in the suits, are designed to get responses.

Successful and I mean really successful salespeople know that after asking a question they must shut up and listen carefully to the answer. But do they listen? I do, sometimes.

But really, why bother asking a question if you don't use the ammunition from the answer? And here we have one of the most important rules not only in selling but in life itself.
Ask, and then listen.

Train yourself to listen to the answers of the questions you ask and only then will you hear your bank account go Cha Ching.

Enthusiasm

You sell toilet paper. You absolutely love your product, it is the best on the market, sells well, puts food on the table and makes your life complete.

After years of selling any inferior crap which came your way, you have finally found a product which has put you on your road to success.

You are totally psyched to go to work every day and spread the word about your perfect product, but remember.

Just because you are crazy enthusiastic about your product and have a tremendous upbeat presentation which exemplifies the superiority of your brand, price and financial benefits to the customer does not mean that your customer will buy 100 cases of toilet paper then run out and have Charmin tattooed on his ass. After all, to him it's just toilet paper.

Enthusiasm in moderation is the key here. While your customer will undoubtedly be happy for you because your life is great, you must remain sensitive to one very important fact.

Even though your toilet paper will leave him with a clean and fresh smelling ass, there is a very good chance that his life will still suck after you leave. So don't overdo it.

Motivation

For this section I am paraphrasing a story that was recently passed along to me which really says it all. I was sitting on a park bench next to a homeless man and started a conversation by asking him how he ended up sleeping on the street.

He said, "Up until last week, I still had it all. There was always plenty to eat and my clothes were clean and pressed. With a roof over my head, I had TV, Internet, and went to the gym and the pool every day to stay in shape.

Then around eleven every morning, you would find me working on my MBA on-line at the library. I had the perfect life with no bills, no debt and even full medical coverage. One day I woke up and just like that, it was over."

I felt sorry for that guy losing everything and asked, "What happened? Was it drugs, booze, divorce?"

"Oh no, nothing like that," he said. "I got out of prison."

Simple fact folks, if they are used to getting it for free as so many are, no matter how they got it, they probably won't ever have the motivation to work for it or pay for it. You need to be very selective in your choosing of prospects as there are only so many selling hours in a day. Don't waste time on guaranteed non buyers.

Right up front, ask the right questions to determine if this is a quality prospect in front of you and if not, move on and find greener pastures. Remember, you can't sell a milkshake to a rock. Yes, I am short on metaphors but done with this subject so just accept the milkshake thing and let's not dwell here any longer.

Perspective

Everyone can look at a situation and come up with a different scenario, approach or result.

Just take the milkshake thing. Yea I know we were done with that but it fits for this subject so work with me here for a sentence or two.

One person might look at the milkshake poured all over the rock and think what a waste of good food with all of the hungry people in the world.

Another person might reflect on the fact that the milkshake is part of the environmental cycle and will nourish the small animals which inhabit the area.

I would say some slob spilled their shit all over that rock and didn't bother to clean it up.

Whatever your mindset you must always remember that there are many varied opinions for every situation and since you can't possibly know what your prospect is thinking, why not ask them?

The perfect example of perspective was passed on to me long ago and I now pass it to you.

The sinking of the Titanic was a horrific tragedy for all of those aboard.

Except for the three lobsters in the kitchen fish tank.

What do you sell again?

Yea we have all been there, three quarters of the way through our presentation when the target looks at you and says "What else do you sell?"

By the time you done calling this guy an asshole the elevator dings and brings you back to the lobby. I'm as guilty as the next guy and it just so happens that you are the next guy.

We have been selling and closing for so long, we forget that even the most tenured customer has other things on his mind besides giving us his undivided attention right from the gun. I know, what a douche, right?

He should be happy that you are there offering him the opportunity to make the next payment on the BMW you just picked up. But for some reason he was unaware or unprepared to assume his role in this sales process, that of robotic buyer.

Could we, the sales rep possibly share in some of the responsibility for this miscommunication? Well, I guess we could eat a little crow. Especially if you're ordering the All Day Breakfast as the ingredients merely say "Meat"

But we have made this pitch a thousand times before and at least twice to that very customer. What in his life could have possibly been important enough to make him forget that?

And here you are assuming that what you do, the first priority of your every business day is also the first priority of his every business day. We are right back to never assuming and asking questions aren't we?

Funny how often we wind up right back at this basic first step but we bring it upon ourselves.

Selling is simply a repetition and numbers game but you can't expect your target to keep track for you.

If I only had a nickel for each time I heard one of my sales people say to a prospect "As you remember from our last discussion," man, I hate that.

If he remembered your last discussion you would have closed the sale the last time.

And besides that how do you know nothing regarding his wants or needs has changed since your last discussion?

For all you know, he could have gone vegetarian last week and you sell meat.

Don't start off where you left off.

Be a professional every time and start with the questions that encourage them to tell you what they are looking for.

Ask, don't assume and increase your rate of Cha Ching

When We Assume

Every day for many years I walked from the subway to my sales territory in lower Manhattan.

Along that three block walk there were a number of retail stores and office buildings. Plus two restaurants, a pizza place and a burger joint, one big commercial bank and an amazing clock store.

And the stand out, was that cool clock store. There were cuckoo clocks on the wall, modern clocks which hung from the ceiling and one great big Grandfather clock right in the middle of them all. I often wished there was room in my apartment for that Grandfather clock but city living meant minimizing.

Anyway, one evening on my walk from work back to the subway, I noticed my watch had stopped. Figuring the battery died, I went into the clock store to have it replaced.

At the counter was an older short man with a pleasant smile and I asked him "Can you put a battery in my watch while I wait?"

He said, "No, I don't fix watches, I'm a Rabbi and I do circumcisions in the back room."

Shocked at his answer I asked him "If you don't fix watches then why do you have all of those clocks in the window?"

He said "Ok, smart guy. You know what I do, so tell me, what should I hang in my window?"

Don't assume. Nuff said.

And I don't understand

Why do the people with the strongest non understandable foreign accents and least command of the English language become receptionists and customer service reps?

Why do people write long emails directly onto a page in an email program and address them first? Why not write it in a program like Word, getting it perfect and then cut and paste it into an email.

You can do this before you accidentally send the misspelled, poorly phrased letter while picking that perfectly good crumb of corn muffin crumb off of the keyboard.

Crap. Did I just send that?

Seriously, my opinion, which I know is only worth the price of this book, is that technology needs to be reverse engineered to keep it simple.

Like, would someone please tell me why we turn off the GPS just before we get to our destination?

Come on, you do it, we all do it. You're a mile away so you turn it off and then a half mile later you hit a traffic circle. You know the type with eleven exits and several missing street signs.

And of course being so close to your destination you're no longer paying attention because Carlos Santana is doing his thing on the radio and your phone is ringing and you just got a text. The next thing you see is a sign saying next exit forty three miles.

Technology is great but it dulls our senses and creates a

dependence which turns off a part of the brain.

Why do people write partial emails anyway? If an email requires a follow-up to explain the first one, I see an issue here.

When I die I'm going to have my lawyer send out the following mass email. "To all of my family and friends, I left the million dollars behind the"

Look sales team, here's the bottom line. If you forget about personal one on one, face to face communication then you subject yourself to disappointment by email.

I'm sure you will agree it is much easier to say no on the phone, in a text or email than in person.

In person they need to look you in the eye, say no, and then answer questions to justify their decision. Thereby creating opportunities to resell and reclose the sale.

These face to face say No confrontations are very tense times indeed which every potential customer tries to avoid. For your target, an email is simply, "Not interested" click. Ok where did I put that jelly donut?

In fact, right now as I write this book I have a customer who blew me off by email. I called him and emailed, faxed and even snail mailed him several times because I realized how busy he was.

Recently I even left a message with the guy who sits in the office next to him. I told the guy in the next office that the targets mailbox was full and I needed to have him call me about his request. Factually correct? Of course not. Did it work? No.

Realizing that no one is that busy and knowing damn well that he indeed received at least one of my attempts to reach him, I reclassified this particular x-customer as a flaming asshole but still hadn't made the effort to get in front of him face to face.

Now I lost this customer to an inferior solution not because it was cheaper but because someone got there to put a pen in his hand. Poor time management on my part combined with giving him credit for knowing we had a better product.

Let's remember the customer won't sell himself and I was so busy doing everything else I expected him to do just that.

Even with all of my excuses, we all know that this lost commission was 100% my fault and this deal went south because I didn't realize my mistakes until it was one stroke of the pen to late.

I harp at my team to stay off of the email, phone and absolutely no texting to customers. (A text does not even create a paper trail like a fax or email) I instruct them to review the "hot list" every day so no one is skipped, to be persistent but not a pest and always try to get face to face with the decision maker. In this case I should have listened to my own advice.

You and I, must frequently take the time to reevaluate our target list and qualify the hot from the cold, prearrange our schedule, have a plan B and ask for the order every time. That's how we professionals increase our incomes. And let's leave the texting to the fourteen year old girls.

I Split My Pants

When you're a fat kid you learn about how things in life are always changing.

You see, back in the 1950's and 1960's way before I became a fat man, I was a fat kid.

Back then in the days of black and white TV, burgers and shakes (part of the problem) and drinking water from the garden hose there was also only one style of pants available at one of the three stores that sold them.

It didn't matter if they were chinos, dungarees (today's jeans) or the single inevitable pair of "dress pants" in your closet, they were all cut to the same shape.

Cut with a high waist, long crotch, and flat ass. They were too long for everyone except Lou Alcindor, oh yea Kareem Abdul Jabir to most of you. He was just about the only one that didn't have to roll up the cuffs.

Well I guess you get the gist of just how long ago it was and how long the pants were.

Anyway, the manufacturers were quite aware that we humans came in all shapes and sizes but conventional wisdom back then was that everyone would cram, squeeze, slide or caress their ass into the generic shaped jeans. And they were right.

To go full circle here, my fat ass was a cross between the squeeze and cram method and after a little wear and a gentile prodding like one good bend over or even a quick flip of my leg over the bicycle seat, there was usually a pronounced ripping sound.

And then suddenly I was a Greek god. U rippa deeze, I fixa deeze. (Sorry old joke that Dr. Dave told me. Some things just stick with you.)

Now it's not that later in life my wife was unhappy about my sewing talents, after all to this day when she needs a quick hem fixed, I'm the go to guy.

Yet as many times as I have tried to explain my sewing prowess, she just doesn't care why or how it gets done and walks away knowing the job will be, like everything else I did, well done.

Wada you mean not everything? It's called poetic license and I'm taking it.

Knowing that you care and or are trapped in this subject until the next chapter, I will be courteous and brief even after your questionable remark.

No, really I can do it.

Let's face reality here. There are those who will accept just about anything if it does the job and those who want only the best fit. Way back when in the black and white TV days just having a TV represented that you were modern and wanted the best.

But in today's Google, Amazon gotta have it right now world, just having it no longer makes you special. Simply ordering something because it's good enough is for the small thinking. It's bucket of ice for your beer on warm day thinking.

In the blink of an eye, forty some odd years, the ice bucket solution dropped from the best thing since well, buckets of ice, to no big deal and just doing the job till it melts.

The best, today, right this minute is a nitrogen generating swizzle stick which instantly chills your drink to the perfect temperature.

It is available only from the manufacturer in Finland. Distributed through your company at a ridiculously high price, and might I say, wait let me lean in closer here, it is in seriously short supply, but I have some in inventory.

Herein lays the challenge. Will your prospect spend the major bucks to have a frozen poker of his own? Or is he the ice will do fine guy because ice always did fine in the past?

Finding this out and selling the appropriate product is where salesmen make their money. Upgrading the guy who wants the $3.00 bucket of ice to the $29.95 swizzle stick freezing device is where great salesmen make even more money.

Getting the guy who you converted to today's technology to tell all his friends about it and you then getting referrals, names and numbers is where amazing salesmen make tons of money.

Want to be amazing? Of course you do what a stupid question. OK, then mystify and amaze all of your prospects with a story, yes you can use mine, it comes with the book.

You need to have a conversation that explains the evolution of your product, enhances not only their knowledge of the subject but enhances their desire to be part of it.

If their driving a Tesla, it immediately looks like a winner for the frozen poker but if their behind the wheel of a 73 beetle with duct tape on the convertible top, it looks like one bucket of ice to go.

But how do you know? Maybe the VW was his dads and gets driven once a month while the new electric BMW is charging in the garage.

Caution, don't prejudge as it will only cost you a sale. Why not just ask for the order on the most expensive first and see if they bite. Worst case scenario you sell the bucket of ice and move on.

Best case, you prove that selling is a numbers game and the more you ask for the big deal, and the less you prejudge the more you Cha Ching your way through life. And that is the goal here more Cha Ching right?

In closing this chapter, see I told you I could be brief, let's all remember, me included, to shut up after each time you ask for the order so you can hear him want to buy it.

Finally (no applause) here is a little story about prejudging.

A penguin was at the auto repair shop waiting for her car to be repaired. She sat patiently in the waiting room happily dipping her beak in a cup of delicious vanilla ice cream which the service writer gave her as a treat while waiting. The mechanic walked over to her and said, "Miss Penguin, it looks like you blew a seal." "No" she said, "I ate an ice cream."

And there you have it, proof positive that questions beat statements and rarely prejudge you out of a sale.

Hey, we're out of coffee.

That can't be, I bought a pound just last week. Wait a minute, this isn't a pound. The label on this can reads eleven point four thirteenths of a pound of coffee. The price is the same so where the hell did the rest of my pound of coffee go?

And this random thought was brought to you by Southwest airlines who just handed me a bag with nineteen peanuts in it.

Yes pour them in your hand and there they are, the entire contents of the bag now fit in even the smallest of hands. And wait a tic, they are all half nuts which means there are only 9.5 peanuts in this bag.

Unlike me, I'm totally nuts, but seriously there's not a whole peanut in the bag.

What? What do you mean their free? I paid $298 dollars for this one way to NY and a flight all the way to Bangladesh should I ever decide to go there, was only $319.

Which raises the question, what is the actual value of an airplane ticket and how much does this tiny bag of nuts effect that price? Yea, I can't figure it out either but back to the point here.

Of course there's a point, I just haven't thought of it yet. Wait, I got it.

Unless you have a captive audience or you're a hypnotist and can get your target to buy from you no matter what the circumstances, you need reasons and justification for those reasons for him to buy regardless of the price or cost of your product. Especially if there is cheaper competition out there, and there almost always is.

You know, I think I want to try something here. You are getting sleepy but not from reading this book. In fact you are enjoying this read so much that you will now go to Amazon and order ten more copies of this book for your salesmen friends. Go ahead, I'll wait.

Did it work? Hummm, didn't think so. Hypnotism is not as good as justification.

Oh, sorry, SNAP.

Right here, right now we have identified one of the most important cornerstones of selling which you need to constantly improve upon. You need to give your target reasons to buy, right now.

Let's remember that many people never split their pants and they are wary of change because they haven't experienced it. Just because their big and fat now doesn't mean they were always big and fat. (I write as I eat the best breakfast at The Town & Country Family Restaurant in Rochester NY. Christina and Nick really got it going on.)

Besides, society has advanced along with the dollar menu to make pants that fit you even if you're shaped like a three hundred pound teardrop.

Now, what if your product hasn't changed in say forever, you had better find out early in the conversation if your target is looking for change. The answer to that question affords you the ability to pick a direction to sell and close on.

If your product is the same as it has always been then you can use the time tested quality and reliability which your company has exhibited since Fred Flintstone stopped the car with his feet.

Or, you can go with something more misdirecting to wrap your targets arms around your product offerings being so accepted to this very day and that major change has never been needed.

"Technology is a wonderful thing, like the electric car which saves the worlds fossil fuels and cleans the air, but it still runs out of juice every eighty miles, ugg. I don't know about you but some things are better left original, like the smell of a fresh cut lawn, a car that can get you to your grandchildren's house a hundred miles away and our product here."

And that's why even though we offer many newer solutions, this product still sits on the top of the heap as our flagship. Mostly because it never requires major changes to do its functions, computer tweaking or even multiple training sessions (or whatever). You see where I'm going here, use every inch of that winding road to the close while opening the discussion of newer choices all available by you.

And when you offer the old and the new in your product line, you need to have reasons to follow the targets lead and close one of your products against the other right then, eliminating the need for him to look at outside competitive products or services. Using the entire range of your products properly totally excludes any consideration of the competitors' products.

It is important however that you do not confuse your target with too many choices.

This could delay the sale and open a window for another salesman to get face to face with him and close because the customer is tired of looking and the competitions product is good enough.

Again, that's where questions and listening come in. He doesn't care about your entire product line but just his needs and you want to fill them right there and then.

Yea it's tougher without the hypnotism, but the success rate is high when you professionally, convincingly present like the master of your product and industry, and suggest solutions based on the following proven process.

Ask the question, shut up and listen, present product with additional questions, shut up and listen, close, shut up and listen, execute contract, shut up and listen, summarize with justification, shut up and listen, shake hands, shut up and walk out the door.

You will notice that the effective sales process is like the local train and success requires many stops.

Remember, if you take the express train you will fly right past all of the opportunities. The opportunity to lock the competition out of the conversation and the opportunity to minimize buyer's remorse giving the customer his justification which he needs to sleep well and send the bean counters down the road when they question his purchase of your products.

The importance of asking questions and then keeping the mouth closed and the ears open is the sign of a true professional.

Yea, it's hard as hell when you ask a question you already know the answer to but have to wait for the answer from a guy who thinks before every word, stutters and slurs what he doesn't stutter.

After more than fifty years selling, I still struggle with it daily.

But silence is golden. The type of gold which goes in your pockets when you ask a question and pay careful attention to the answer, act accordingly then ask for the order.

It's my stop. I have made my point so ill shut up now.

I Like Mine Shiny

Imagine you are in New York City riding on the bus looking at the big buildings towering all around you. Apartment buildings office buildings, stores, restaurants and shops, endlessly flowing buy one after another after another.

You just can't stop wondering how all of this came to be, also how successful most of those entrepreneurial spirits must have become creating all of this. But what you're really wondering is, how do I become one of those success stories today? Good question.

Let's try to figure it out together and start by traveling back in time to Ellis Island, the entry point to America for so many immigrants arriving from 1892 to 1924. When they walked off of their final boat ride to the USA they were greeted by a New York City much different than where your bus is currently dropping off passengers a century later.

Where that shoe store is over there was a forest and by the Starbucks, that was a swamp. And your bus route for today, 2nd Avenue in Manhattan was nothing but a dirt road just wide enough for a logger's wagon to traverse. (But I do think the pot holes you just hit are original)

Anyway, since most of the new comers traveled together, naturally they settled together in groups, hence Spanish Harlem, Chinatown, Little Italy etc.

One such new comer, we will call Geppetto came from a small town in Italy and made his living as a craftsman with wood. Since he had seven brothers also named Geppetto who arrived with him, for his new life in his new country he used his nick name, Tosh.

His seven brothers used their last name Santini and became famous in their own right.

But back to our story, another guy living in the neighborhood down the street named Andrezej was originally from the apple orchards in the Southern hills of Poland and back home they called him Mackie.

Since they both just arrived and most of the available jobs were saved for friends and relatives by those who arrived before them, getting a job was very hard at best.

Neither one of these guys had any contacts, money or promises, so they each went out walking the street seeking opportunity. (No, Obama wasn't there to give them everything.)

Then it happened. These two strangers, sitting on the grass under an apple tree begin to talk. And that's how a great new business idea came to life.

Andrezej says that he used to grow apples and if he had a way to transport them, he would pick the apples from this tree right here and sell them on the corner of his street.

After all, there were plenty of hungry workers building apartments and putting up street lights and such to be his customers. Then he said, soon he would buy an orchard upstate and go into the apple business in a big way. That was his idea of the American dream.

Geppetto said that he could build a fine cart out of the scrap lumber from the construction underway in his neighborhood. And then they could push that cart under this tree where together they could pick apples at night and then push the cart place to place as a moving store and sell them to all of the workers. American dream times two.

And just that quickly, one of the first new world partnerships was created and they combined their nick names calling the business the Mackie Tosh Apple Cart Company. Catchy name, huh?

Geppetto made a sign "Fresh from the tree Apples" and business took off like wildfire.

Soon they had three people picking apples for them and found the absolute best corner with the most foot traffic to set up their store. Hungry people were happily paying a penny an apple (The equivalent of today's $2,675,381.99 with inflation and National Debt calculated in.) and they sold out of inventory every day.

Just an FYI, foot traffic alone does not promise results. You must do research before you decide on a location. I think I proved that with my failed pulled pork lunch cart in front of the Mosque.

Anyway, everything was going well for our boys when all of a sudden there appeared another apple business across the street. Now they didn't have a nice rolling cart but were selling apples off of a table made from crates and an old plank of wood.

And at the same penny an apple, even though it was just a small table with a father and son running it, just being there they were taking business away from our boys. The inevitable competition had reared its ugly head.

Now any businessman would react to this new attack on their pocketbook. Most of them would quickly start a price war and reduce their price to say 2 apples for a penny.

This price reduction may bring the pennies back but you would need to pay your three tree pickers more to fill the newly required volume so where's the profit? Welcome to the world of business in 1907.

And the problem grows as Mackie and Tosh were sitting over a mug of apple cider talking about their next move, yet another table popped up. They were selling grapes and cherries then another was selling carrots, further reducing the pennies available to spend on their apples.

After all, there are only so many pennies at the market and the more available choices the fewer will usually come your way. Sound familiar?

Before you know it there was an entire fruit and vegetable market flourishing where there once stood your lone MackieTosh apple business.

After seeing the rapid change in their surroundings and marketplace and feeling the effect on their pockets, our boys made the decision to diversify. It was time for Tosh to bring his woodworking skills back into play.

In the evening while their three pickers were getting tomorrow's inventory, Mackie and Tosh were busy collecting scrap lumber from construction sites.

They worked hard fashioning beautiful tables, carved signs and strong chairs to sell to all of the other vendors on the street. And yet another business was born.

The vendors happily trashed their old boxes and planks, which the boys took and reused in the construction of new tables. And while Mackie ran the apple cart Tosh sold, delivered and collected daily payments from his growing list of furniture buyers.

Soon, our boys had a nice steady stream of income which far out produced any money they could make from their shrinking apple business but knew they were still missing something.

With the apple stand location they had staked out a prime piece of real estate in a busy marketplace and also established a reputation as a place to acquire quality furniture.

The news had already spread where others could come to order their tables and such but they needed to find a way to keep the apple business profitable on its own or they were not going to have any money left over after increasing business costs for apple inventory or orchard rental.

After all, when one product wins and one loses that's the true profit killer and you're not going anywhere but out of business.

It's kind of like selling more and more of your products at discounted prices. You are depleting your availability of buyers and reducing your profit on each sale. Do you want fries with that?

Over a piece of hot apple pie they brainstormed looking for a way to keep their core money maker product, apples, profitable even amongst the ever growing number of competitive vendors.

Tosh was holding an apple, tossing it from hand to hand when he dropped it on the ground. Rubbing it clean with his shirt tail yet another miracle of business happened. He stumbled upon product innovation and improvement.

As Tosh rubbed, the apple turned clean and shiny with a beautiful vibrant red color. That same apple they had sold as "fresh from the tree" with a flick of the wrist transformed into a new product. The "shinny apple" was created.

BTW, our boys had rented a small barn on a farmer's field next to the apple orchard in which they built furniture and stored apples and also negotiated exclusive rights to the apples in the orchard.

Late into the evening Mackie and Tosh were sitting polishing apples for their grand new product announcement at the market the next morning.

Tosh was making the sign which read Shiny New Apples when in sheer exhaustion they both admitted that they had bit off more than they could chew. This shiny apple idea was a lot of work and they needed more help to make it a reality.

But more laborers meant more money and after a quick but worrisome conversation they decided the only way to bring their beautiful shiny apples to market was to charge Two Cents each.

What a risk, charging double the price of any other apple at the market.

But they knew that the people in the market were there to buy and hoped that a good number of them were more interested in quality and innovation than price.

And it worked, proving that even back then there were people willing to pay more money for quality products. Why there were even rumors of the other cheaper apples having worms (it wasn't me)

Mackie found a few laborers who worked orchards in their old lands and brought them into the business to pick, polish and pack. With this additional experience and efficiency they had a consistent quality product.

Quickly, with their controlled cost and consistent supply of this exclusive product, sales volume grew and allowed them to open more Mackie Tosh retail locations. Advanced production methods gave them the ability to produce many more shiny apples and also supply other vendors at wholesale. They charged other vendors four cents for three shiny apples totally taking over the quality market segment.

Plus their expanded retail locations which were selling shiny apples in different parts of the city also added additional growth to the furniture business.

As business goes, several profitable years later a grinding stone manufacturer named Mott bought the apple business for his son and well, the rest is applesauce.

So what is it that this nearly, possibly, could be accurate depiction of business creation and evolution tells us?

1st- There is opportunity everywhere. Do not wait for someone else to tell you where to take your stand and create your own success. No soliciting signs are for the other guys.

2nd- There are like minded individuals who are either seeking to create with you or compete against you. If you need to partner up, do so with a company, sales manager, product and philosophy which are in line with your own. Having restrictions on how much you can earn through your efforts and success is a limitation which you alone reserve the right to place upon yourself.

3rd- There are buyers out there who are interested in quality and willing to pay for it. Look team, prices are like opinions, everyone has one. Justify your sale through whichever distinguishing factor makes it worth the price. Bigger, better, colder, hotter anything but cheaper.

4th- And most important, it takes balls as big as the King of Bayonne to get out there and make it happen. Don't wait for the phone to ring, make it ring. Be the customer's unexpected knock on the door. Be the innovative voice of reason and reasonable expectations with which your prospects become customers and better yet, customers who give referrals.

In other words - Get to work.

Ride the Wave

To Close or Not to Close, what kind of a stupid question is that? Good thing Shakespeare wrote plays and didn't sell anything.

Team, let's restate the obvious here. Selling is all about closing and the simplest way to succeed is to be convinced that you can and must close every sale, every time.

Here are perfect examples of factors involved in both closing and not closing the same sale.

Scenario 1 – You are a jewelry salesman and close a guy on a 4 carat $12,000 Marquis Diamond engagement ring.

After several trial closes you were successful by offering him the either or close on that Marquis or Solitaire stone. You limited his selection to utilizing the intelligence gathered during the probing portion of the sale.

While probing and selling the features and benefits of each stone you found out she had long slender fingers and assisted him in visualizing that long Marquis shape fitting perfectly on her hand.

He imagined with you how the stone would add size and dimension. The brilliant stone would be filling her whole finger and be exactly what she would love to have, along with him forever.

How would you like to pay for that?

This was all that was needed to close the deal after this masterful sales presentation then he whips out his Amex and pays for it on the spot.

A job well done, everyone is happy. Thanking you over and over and in his obvious excitement shaking your hand three times he bolts from the store and takes it home to his girl.

She says yes and everyone is happy. He got the ring and the girl and best of all you got the commission. Yes, another fairytale ending, created by the perfect sales presentation.

But things don't always go according to plan so let's look at Scenario 2

You fail to close and the guy holds off on buying a 4 carat $12,000 diamond engagement ring. He tells you he has to think about it and then while he does the dinner dishes he thinks it's a good idea to open a conversation and ask his future bride for her help choosing a shape.

He wants to ask her if she thinks she would like a Solitaire or Marquis shaped stone because after all, he doesn't want to make a mistake and wants her to really, really love it.

Now all of this is entirely your fault because you, the not so professional salesman, didn't help him to make the decision for her as you should have during your feature heavy non closing presentation.

With little intelligence gathering and almost no interactive questions asked, you could not make a convincing argument for either shape of stone helping him make a choice right then.

The lack of questions and worse the lack of interactive questions leading to conversations left you with few clues offered from your excited, confused and now undecided walking out the door meal ticket.

Yes, he walked out of that door without the ring and worse, you let him leave with your commission. It happens every day, you can't write this stuff I tell ya, well I can so here it goes.

You failed to close and the guy holds off on buying a 4 carat $12,000 diamond engagement ring but he does give you something.

He gives you a promise.

He promised right to your face with total sincerity that he would be back first thing tomorrow once she decides on the shape of the ring that she wants. He even asks what time the store opens.

Good intentions? There is no commission paid on good intentions.

That evening at home you are eating dinner all excited because you have a big sale coming in tomorrow. In fact, you imagine at that very moment he is home drying the dinner dishes and asking her about the ring.

He says, "Pumpkin, in your diamond engagement ring, which is the token of my true and everlasting love for you, would you like the stone to be a Solitaire or Marquis?"

But in reality, after he asks that very question, out of nowhere with only that simple question for provocation she embarks on a journey, unexplained throughout time and mankind, freaking out as only a female can.

Not just any average hormonal female emotional outburst but a tirade with the level of pent up pre, mid and post menstrual verbal abuse typically reserved for when the store doesn't have the shoes in her size and she just can't imagine living without them. (Trust me on this one)

This woman is now a tightly wrapped storm just looking for a tear in the seam and once this tear is found the vengeance escapes with wild abandon.

The poor slob asked what he thought was a simple and wonderful question and was expecting a loving response. Instead, it was the question which split the seam and out it came, raging like a storm at sea, dangerous, wild and without warning.

She starts verbally beating on him like a rented mule, berating him with more and more heated question after question and accusation after accusation.

"Diamond? You want to get me a diamond? Can you guarantee it is definitely a conflict free diamond? Did you check the origin? Do you know? Do you even care?"

She continues with "are you like totally aware of the living conditions and plight those poor people endure to collect those stones just so we can have adornment on our hands?"

Story note - You think those conditions are bad? You should try wearing that full length black coat and big hat in the summer in NYC on 47th Street. Just ask my jeweler, Oy vey, hot, hot he'll tell you.

She continues her verbal onslaught with the stamina of a vulture circling its prey until death is welcomed. His torture goes on late into the night as he stands over the sink carefully hand washing her outfit for tomorrows anti Trump rally.

A tie-dyed peace sign ordained halter top made of organic hemp and by the time he is done washing it he will be wishing he could dry out the shirt and smoke the hemp allowing her voice to fade into a blur of weed induced pleasure.

Whoa there, sorry about the mind drifting for a minute.

Admittedly I have inhaled, repeatedly, but I'm not running for president though I have some great ideas and would love to receive the Nobel Prize for good intentions.

Man, I would kill for a Nobel Peace prize, drifting again sorry, ok back to the story.

So there he is, deeply in love and concerned that his token ($12K, some token right?) of love should be everything it needs to be.

But this crazy bitch is standing over him dictating how buying a blood stone is the most terrible crime against humanity and how she couldn't bear to carry the reminder and burden of that horrible inhuman tragedy with her at all times just to wear a ring.

Then just when he thought the storm had finally passed she spends another fifteen minutes making it abundantly clear to him what an insensitive asshole he must be to not think of the world effect directly related to his uneducated purchase.

Then she tells him that he should always think about others before he spends his money.

But hopefully not all of his money because after the rally downtown against white privilege and minimum wage restrictions there is a giant shoe sale and she needs cash for two or three pairs.

OK guys, now I know I'm thinking what he's thinking which is, "I've always wanted to have someone to hold and someone to love. Now that I've met you, I've changed my mind." Then he saved himself $12k by not buying the ring.

Under the circumstances we could forgive this guy for not coming in to buy the ring. But we need to finish this lesson which would have prevented the lost sale in the first place so we continue.

There are salespeople out there who think people are genuinely truthful and if he said he would be back tomorrow with $12k, nothing could possibly change that. Both you and the target think that life is simple, she will pick a shape and he will be there to pay.

In this salespersons own naive little world he is sure that when tomorrow comes, the guy will come strolling back in with a credit card waiving in the air and buy one of the 4 carat $12,000 diamond engagement rings.

Yeah, he pictures it vividly in his mind but is this what life has really got in store for him the next day?

At nine in the morning, there he is the anxious sales guy. Sitting by the jewelry store door he knows that guy will come bounding in early because he was really genuinely excited about getting engaged.

This salesman feels he did such a great sales job explaining the features of both diamonds that all the customer needed was to ask her a simple question and the sale was closed. The target would quickly and easily find out which shape she likes and he would be right back in first thing to buy it.

In his fairytale mind, he believes this is a done deal, solid sale. But the customer has yet to show and now it's almost noon and the salesman begins to question himself. Over and over again and again he wonders where is this guy?

It's getting late but he figures he had better skip lunch after all he wouldn't want to miss this customer and risk losing such a big deal.

He figures that there must be a lot of traffic or limited parking because of some 5k run or parade or something going on today.

Hey there's a half-eaten Twinkie in the drawer anyone mind if I eat it?

Four o'clock, what the fuck? Starving and pissed off and all he sold all day was two watch batteries and a gold plated cross on lay a way. Where the hell is the guy for this diamond ring?

At six p.m. the boss yells across the store, closing time and turns out the lights. Reality is that this salesman didn't make one thin dime on this guy in love and its 100% his own dam fault.

I see you all nodding your heads in agreement. (Speaking figuratively here, I can't really see you. It's ok to read my books in the bathroom. Honest.)

Where did this guy screw up the sale and why didn't he close? Put yourself in this salesman's shoes and feel his big mistake.

Simply put, he was not riding the wave. For this emotional sale, the customer needs to be in love with you the salesman, not her. He was already in love with her when he walked in to the store.

It was the salespersons job to capitalize on this guys weakened condition, agree with his decision to get married, also be in love with her (if she's into that sort of thing) and give him what he wants and needs right there and then.

It's the same thing if he loved fishing and you sold fishing poles or he loved cars and you helped him decide on a color.

This guy in love needs help spending his money, so help him decide what's best for him and for God's sake take his money.

Even this example of a poor henpecked destined for a lifetime of misery piece of shit excuse for a man who had money to spend yet who never came back in to buy a ring would have benefited greatly from a professional selling closer.

Had the salesman done his job and closed this jamoke right then, when he walked in to the house with that big ass 4 carat rock of any shape to put on her finger he would have gotten right past all of that hippy, socialist, bloodstone save the world bullshit.

With his new found confidence, a bottle of Jack in his hand and that compressed piece of carbon on her finger, he would have grabbed her and bent that bitch over the sink yelling at the top of his lungs "let's get married." as she was throwing dishes and screaming "Yes" at the top of hers.

I call that driving home the essence of capitalism.

Man, I just love selling.

I asked my secretary for some mathematical help. I asked her if I gave you $14,800 minus 12% how much would you take off.

She said everything but my diamond earrings. Sure as hell makes you want to be the guy selling the diamonds, don't it?

By the way, I have yet to meet a woman who doesn't love a diamond and if you do meet one please let me know because I got stuck with a couple of cubic zirconium.

What can I say, I was traveling abroad and it looked real enough to me, he was really quite a great salesman and I kind of got caught up in the moment.

Ok, no more fantasies, back to our serious topics of selling and earning. Remember that no one cares about you earning a living but you. No one will hand you anything, you need to earn it.

A guy walked up to me on the street and said. "I haven't had anything to eat in 3 days". I said "I wish I had your willpower."

Anyway, ask yourself, besides selling what would you do?

Once when my confidence in my sales abilities was low I tried being a life guard, but then some blue kid got me fired.

The science of selling, and don't let anybody fool you, it is a science, is all about the close.

Team, your job is not to present, not to ask questions and not to convince anybody of anything. Those are merely steps and tools you use to do your one and only job.

Ira Levofsky

Close the deal.

Your first question in any sales situation can simply be "How would you like to pay?"

The serious buyer might just say cash or finance.

The serious but undecided buyer might ask "how can I pay?" Then an instant close of course is the either or on cash or finance.

Weeding out the shoppers from the buyers should happen right up front in every sales situation.

Remember that unlike the actor in the play who got paid up front from ticket sales, when the curtain goes down on your sales opportunity you need the deal closed, in hand or you just gave a free performance.

To Close or Not to Close, what kind of a stupid question is that?

The Roar of the Engine

My first car was a twice handed down and very used Black 1966 Chevy II with a six cylinder engine, continuous thirst for oil and a questionable battery.

And no matter what I did, there was just no way to turn that old car into one of the rumbling monsters many of the other kids were rolling through the old neighborhood.

But as a young kid wanting to belong, I tried my best by adding a Cherry Bomb glass pack muffler and applying some STP stickers.

Making some noise plus having some of the same colors and logos on my fenders was as close as I could come to the big car guys on the street but in the eyes of the average bystander I was one of those guys with a cool car because I looked and sounded kind of like them.

Now you're probably mumbling to yourself, how the hell is he going to transition to something I care about and even more importantly when?

The answers are, easy and now.

Think back to your own life experiences for a minute. You watch a baseball or basketball game and there's always one guy, be it a kid or a pro, which just by the look on his face is doing the thing he loves most in life to do.

Simply look past the face mask on a football helmet of that human freight car who almost took the head off of the runner with the ball. That's not playing a game of football, but the love of playing that you see in his eyes.

Perhaps the most telling lesson in my life was while watching a Broadway musical and noticing while the fake smiles were bright and wide, you could still see the concentration and exacting effort on the face of the dancers.

All but the one or two who stood out and seemed like they were floating effortlessly through their private fantasy land.

Just like a plastic bag in the Walmart parking lot, no thought involved, just happening naturally from the wind. There that woke your senses up didn't it?

There are those who need to try and those that need only to do, which is which is quite obvious to everyone in the audience.

When you are selling, others are watching you perform. Like my big brother reminded me of again just today, talk only about what you know.

If you dwell into areas that are uncertain or uncomfortable for you and get challenged by someone who actually knows what they are talking about, you get nervous and even if your answers are correct you could lose the deal because you are thinking too much and the customer senses that.

I know it sounds crazy but when you think too hard, you are telegraphing much more than what you are saying. The wrinkles, squinting and air of uncertainty ring like a bell. And you can never un-ring the sound of a bell.

Granted, we can't learn every aspect of every product in our sales bags but the odds are pretty good that your target knows what they themselves are looking for so why not just ask them.

Simply ask them what their looking for and then give, get or find them their information which puts you solidly into your comfort zone of presenting and closing on what you have rock solid experience with and not scratching through your knowledge base for bits and pieces of information.

After all, you didn't spend eight years in engineering school and then fifteen years practicing their trade so you shouldn't be expected to know all of the answers.

You are expected to be the supplier with basic knowledge and arrangement of payment and delivery. The customer chooses what they want to buy. Here is a real life example again by virtue of my brother telling me to try not to be an asshole.

At my company, we have a new piece of equipment which has a 440 CFM pump. What the hell does that mean and just how much is a CFM?

My brother's suggestion was to find out how many cubic feet of water is in an Olympic swimming pool (which I did with Google.) Divide that number by 440 and you will have the amount of time it takes for your pump to empty it. A nice general feature and benefit statement showing some familiarity with the product regardless of your or their depth of knowledge.

As it turns out, with this new equipment we could pump out and empty an entire in ground pool in just over three and a half hours. Pretty impressive when I found out that it takes days to fill the same pool with a garden hose.

Now I have a simple story my sales team can tell, backed with two very cool but simple photographic sales tools. One shot of the equipment with the pump and one of a pool full of water.

Add to the exchange a simple question like "How much stuff do you need to pump?" and his engineering mind will do the rest.

Show and tell so you can just keep doing the thing you love without to much thinking and no guessing. Telling a story and gaining involvement with interactive conversation will make the purchase as fulfilling to the customer as the sale is to you.

Helping the target put all of the puzzle pieces together but not doing it for them is the key.

Your target is talking with you because they are curious. Or they want to buy and need a little help being pushed over the edge of the decision. They don't want to be sold. Let them have their way. Let them buy.

They are not talking with you because their bored and if they are you will know that from the first questions you ask and then you bail out of there and find a serious buyer.

Do what you love to do and allow your target to share in the experience culminating with a signature, a curtain call and then exit stage left.

By the way, even though I run the sales force for companies, my responsibilities always involve working a territory and meeting a quota. I don't believe anyone can stay in touch with their marketplace sitting behind a desk.

Does Your Prospect Really Want it?

I mean do they want it as bad as you want them to have it?

Here you need to really read the signals, body language, verbal including inflection of the words and energy put into motions and actions.

This might be one of the most difficult parts of the sale but to become a master at selling you must learn to pay attention to every detail.

I offer the following example.

One day in Bueafort Alabama, I happened into a small country general store. They sold everything from toilets and ice cream to chewin tobacca.

The sign on the front counter said "Court in Session" and through the partially open door to the back room I witnessed my best ever example of "just how bad you want it and how creative can you get to make it happen?"

Sitting next to the judge in the witness chair was a young woman maybe twenty five years old. In the front row was a man who I found out later was her husband and two little children maybe six or seven years old. All of them were crying their eyes out.

The judge asked "Mam, did you steal that can of peaches?" And through her tears she said "Yes your honor I did." The husband hugged the kids.

The judge then asked "Mam, why did you steal those peaches?" And the woman whimpered "Cause I was hungry." And the kids cried out loud.

Then the judge asked, "How many peaches were in the can?" And the woman fought back the tears and said "Four"

"Then you will spend four nights in jail" the judge said loudly as he slammed his gavel onto the desk. Just then, the husband raised his hand and said

"Judge, I would like to make a statement on my wife's behalf, you see your honor, to be truthful, she also stole a can of corn."

Now he really wanted it.

I had a Doctor's appointment

He told me that the thing he liked best about me was my happy, positive and uplifting personality.

I told him that I was a salesman and spent all day imposing my will on others and helping them do what's best for them while I made money doing it.

He said that he had many patients who were in sales but they were not as engaged with life as I was.

I told him that I also had a new 27 year old girlfriend and it probably helped with my demeanor.

With a stern voice and raised eyebrow he said "Ira, I need to be very honest with you. At sixty one years old and in your physical condition, sex with a girl more than half your age could be fatal."

To which I said "Doc, let me make this as easy to understand and politically correct as possible. If it kills her, it kills her."

And I say the same to you. Close the deal, it won't kill them.

Good Luck and Good Selling

Ira

Read and enjoy all of my books and help keep me in a nice warm climate.

Adventures of Sparky Trilogy
Search for the Butterfly Tattoo
Fortune Cookies Don't Lie
The Pirate Wore Wooden Shoes

Sales
Dinosaur Droppings – Advice From an old-school salesman
Occupy This – Close That Sale
The Sale is Closed – Stop Talking

Specialty
Recovering From Heart- Surgery. Going Home (English)

Recuperandose de una cirugia del corazone Volviendo a casa (Spanish Edition)

www.ingramcontent.com/pod-product-compliance
Lightning Source LLC
Chambersburg PA
CBHW051710170526
45167CB00002B/606